# GROW
## SOMETHING
## DIFFERENT
### TO EAT

# GROW
## SOMETHING
## DIFFERENT
### TO EAT

## MATTHEW BIGGS

# Contents

# Introduction

In our increasingly connected world, we are regularly introduced to exciting new cuisines and unfamiliar foods from across the globe. We are eager to recreate that dish we enjoyed at a restaurant last night, taste again those amazing fruits we discovered on vacation, or try out that new superfood we read about online.

At the same time, more and more of us are breaking free from supermarket conformity and the limited choices offered by industrial-scale food production. We are discovering once again the joys of diversity in fruits and vegetables, and unearthing forgotten crops from closer to home.

Our eyes have been opened to a new world of previously unknown food crops with exciting flavors and often supercharged health benefits. Yet it can be a struggle to find the right ingredients, and where they are available, they can often be prohibitively expensive.

So what should you do? Well, you can grow your own! And thankfully, another benefit of our globalized world is that so many exotic and obscure crops are now widely available to buy as seeds, tubers, and container-raised plants.

By growing your own incredible edibles, not only will you reap the mental and physical benefits of gardening–fresh air, relaxation, and gentle exercise–but the crops you harvest will be at their peak of quality, full of flavor and packed with nutrients. And you can grow them in the quantities you desire, turning a superfood treat into an everyday delight.

The opportunity to grow crops is open to everyone, no matter what little space you have. Whether in pots on a windowsill, in containers on a balcony, in a courtyard allotment, or in a tiny strip of a garden, from inner city to suburb, there is always room to grow your own.

And don't be discouraged if you've never gardened before. With a little attention, most of the crops in this book are easy to grow, and all come with detailed step-by-step instructions and advice. For the absolute beginners among you, I've provided a crash course in cultivating plants in the *Tips and techniques for growing* section.

Whatever your level of experience, I believe everyone should try to grow one or two new crops a year. One of the joys of being alive is finding something new to get excited about. With 58 remarkable crops to discover in the pages of this book, don't just grow and eat the same old thing–grow something different!

Matthew Biggs

# Tips and techniques for growing

Take time to understand your growing space and the conditions needed by each crop, so you can select what will flourish and prepare the ground. Then it's a matter of sowing or planting, tending to the needs of the crops as you watch them grow, and reaping the delicious rewards.

## Deciding what to grow

Faced with so many fascinating options, you probably want to try growing them all, but it's worth pausing to consider the following questions. Be practical in assessing what you can manage, and then browse through the crop choosers on pp.14–19 to help you decide.

The **lavender flowers** of society garlic are both beautiful to look at and powerfully flavored.

### What would I like to grow?

**Crops for the table**  It sounds obvious, but grow crops that you are keen to eat. Use the Cook's tips panels to match crops to your tastes. Those that are unavailable or expensive in stores, or that simply taste better freshly picked, are especially worth growing.

**Crops for the eye**  Every edible plant has aesthetic appeal, too. Plan to create displays of contrasting leaf color and texture, bold flowers, shapely fruits, and architectural form.

### Do I have enough space?

**Grow in pots**  Limited space? No soil? Containers are the answer. Given drainage holes and space for roots, anything can be grown in pots. Square containers make efficient use of space, and those with handles or wheels can be moved from sun to shade.

**Grow up**  Use vertical space by training climbing plants up walls, fences, and other supports.

**Grow indoors**  Use a windowsill to raise seedlings. Given sunlight and large pots, many of the tender crops in this book will happily grow indoors.

**Catch-crop**  Sow fast-growing crops between those that germinate slowly, or hardier crops while waiting to plant out tender crops.

**Work in edibles**  Find space in existing ornamental borders to grow edibles. Perennial crops and shrubs can make attractive permanent features.

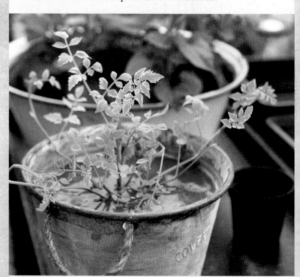

**If you don't have a pond,** grow water-loving crops such as water celery in a metal container.

### Do I have the time and inclination?

**Start small**  There's no need to aim for perfection or self-sufficiency. It's better to enjoy growing a few crops well than have the burden of maintaining too many. Grow more as you gain experience.

**Little and often**  Even the busiest people can find time to grow edibles. The key to keeping on top of things is to check plants and carry out jobs as frequently as you can. And there are numerous time-saving techniques (see *Reduce your workload*, opposite).

**Horticultural fleece** protects plants from frost, as well as pests such as caterpillars.

**Consider growing** in raised beds if drainage or soil quality is poor.

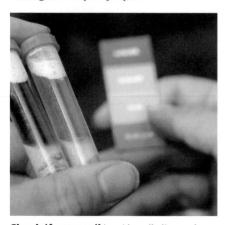

**Check if your soil** is acid or alkaline and tailor your planting accordingly.

## Do I have the right growing conditions?

**General climate** Plants that hail from a climate similar to your own are more likely to thrive with minimal input. Cooler areas have a shorter frost-free growing season, so outdoor sowing is done later and tender crops may need protection to reach maturity. Latitude also affects day length, which influences when some crops will be ready to harvest.

**Sun and shade** Edible crops generally prefer full sun, so note how much sun your garden gets during the day and at different times of year, and choose the sunniest spot for them. Make use of heat radiating from sunny walls.

**Wind and frost** Both make growing difficult and should be avoided as much as possible. Wind damages plants and chills the ground, while frost lingers in shady corners and at the bottom of slopes, and can kill off seedlings and tender plants. Use shelter from existing walls or trees, and add a permeable barrier, like a hedge, to allow cold air to drain through.

**Rainfall** In regions with low rainfall, and where soil is dry at the base of walls and fences, installing drip irrigation provides a consistent supply of moisture. Digging in organic matter, such as garden soil, will improve the moisture-holding capacity of soil. Where rainfall is high, raised beds improve drainage.

**Soil type** Soil composition influences how it drains and holds nutrients. All soils benefit from the addition of organic matter, and you can improve the drainage of clay soil by digging in horticultural sand or grit. Check whether your soil is acid, alkaline, or neutral with a simple pH test kit. If it is highly acidic, add lime to increase the pH and grow acid-loving plants like the tea shrub. Where soil is poor or full of broken stone, the easiest solution is to create raised beds or grow in containers.

## Reduce your workload

Don't waste time in the garden with unnecessary work. Try these top labor-saving tips:

- Plant through a plastic mulch or apply a thick organic mulch around plants (above) to reduce the need for weeding and watering.
- Plant densely to crowd out weeds.
- Buy annuals as young plants if you have no time to raise from seed.
- Grow perennial crops, such as skirret and Chilean guava, which are usually less work than annuals.
- Install an automatic drip irrigation system (below) to save watering; this is especially useful for containers.

continued »

# Growing from seed

Growing your own plants from seed is satisfying and fun: you will never lose the childlike pleasure of seeing the first green shoots peeping through the soil. It is also easy to do if you follow the step-by-step guides so that each crop is given the conditions it needs to get off to the best start. Investing in specialty equipment, such as a heated propagator and soil thermometer, is worthwhile and improves the chance of success.

**Smaller seeds** can be sown thickly in shallow trays but must be potted up individually as soon as they can be handled.

**Sow large seeds** in individual pots filled with potting mix, inserting one seed per pot and covering it over.

## Sowing indoors

Indoor sowing can be done anywhere light and warm, such as on a windowsill or in a greenhouse. It's a great way to give hardy crops a head start and extend the growing season for tender crops in colder climates. Sow into clean containers filled with good-quality garden soil or organic seed-starting mix. Water with lukewarm tap water and keep in a lidded propagator (ideally heated) at 64–68°F (18–20°C), unless instructions state otherwise.

**Sowing small seeds** Fill a shallow seed tray with potting mix. Mix the seeds with fine dry sand and sow thinly over the surface. Sift a thin layer of potting mix or vermiculite over the seeds and water using a watering can with a fine rose. Once large enough to handle, transplant the seedlings into larger pots or cellular trays by easing the roots out with a dibble and holding the seed leaves.

**Sowing larger seeds** For medium-sized seeds, sow 2 seeds per module of a cellular tray or root-trainer, cover lightly with potting mix, and water. Once germinated, remove the weakest seedling, then transplant when the first roots are visible through drainage holes in the base. Sow and transplant large seeds in the same way, but sow individually into 3½in (9cm) pots by pressing them down into the potting mix.

## Heated propagators

Constant heat produces the quickest, most reliable germination, and it is worth investing in a heated propagator for early sowing, as temperatures in unheated propagators and on top of refrigerators and dryers fluctuate. Buy one large enough to suit your needs, ideally with a digital thermostat for accurate temperature control and even germination; the cost will be repaid through less wasted seed and at harvest time.

## Acclimatizing plants

If you have ever jumped into a cold bath, then you'll know what it's like for a young plant taken straight from a greenhouse to a cold, breezy vegetable plot: the shock is enough to check growth or even kill it. Plants raised under cover must be acclimatized gradually in a process called "hardening off."

**How to harden off**

**Week 1**–Leave seedlings outside during the day covered with 2 layers of fleece. Bring in at night.

**Week 2**–Reduce to 1 layer of fleece. Near the end of the week, remove fleece during the day and, if it's not too cold, leave plants out at night but covered.

**Week 3**–Toward the end of the week, leave uncovered day and night before planting out. Be ready with fleece if frost is forecast.

**Alternatively**, place plants in a cold frame–a wooden box with a hinged glass lid–and prop the lid open during the day, progressively wider, then shutting it again at night, until the lid is left fully open day and night in week 3.

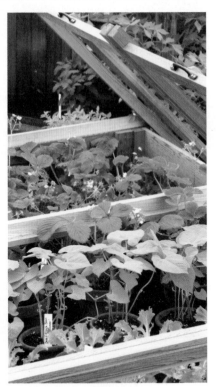

**A cold frame** is a useful structure for hardening off young plants.

## Sowing outdoors

Seed can also be sown directly outdoors into a prepared seedbed. React to the weather each season rather than relying on seed packet instructions for when to sow. Seeds will not germinate in cold, wet weather. Wait until the soil is warm and moist–invest in a soil thermometer to check–and germination will be quicker and more consistent.

**Prepare the seedbed** Improve the soil as described on the next page, then level it by raking in two directions at 90 degrees. Cover with plastic to warm and hoe off any weed seedlings.

**Sow in drills** Rake again before sowing. Make a drill by drawing along the corner of a rake. Water the drill before sowing, and sprinkle seed thinly into the bottom. Lightly cover with soil and label with the plant's name and the date of planting.

**As you rake**, remove debris, such as large and medium stones.

## Sourcing seeds

All the unusual crops in this book are available from seed merchants and specialty suppliers on the internet, but explore other sources, too. Chickpeas, fenugreek, taro, amaranth, and turmeric can be found in Asian grocers, while society garlic and hostas are grown by specialty nurseries. Save seed from your own crops by allowing them to flower and shaking the dry pods or seedheads into a paper bag or envelope in summer. Then take part in "seed swaps," which are a great chance to meet and chat with enthusiastic growers and discover something new. I first discovered achocha and an amaranthus simply labeled 'Tower Hamlets' (a borough of London, England) at a seed swap.

continued »

# Planting and general care

Moving new plants to their final positions is a satisfying moment. To help them establish quickly, it's important to prepare the growing site properly and plant out new arrivals with care. Plants grown in open soil are often good at looking after themselves, but a little regular watering, feeding, and weeding will spur them on. Don't forget that crops in pots and under cover are totally reliant on you for water and nutrients.

## Preparing the site

Make life easy for yourself by providing crops with their preferred soil conditions. Most crops love a moisture-retentive, free-draining soil with an open structure full of airy spaces, a bit like a bath sponge.

**Improving the soil** Clear the site of weeds and remove any larger stones and other debris before digging in plenty of well-rotted organic matter, such as manure, growing medium, or leaf mold. Spread it thickly over the planting site and then thoroughly mix into the soil using a garden fork. Heavy clay will also benefit from the addition of sharp sand or horticultural grit and gypsum to improve drainage. Give the soil a few days to settle before planting.

**Using raised beds** Easy to maintain and a great way to bring in good soil where yours is poor, raised beds can be built very simply using recycled scaffolding boards or similar planks fitted in place with stakes.

■ Leave access paths between beds.

■ Orient east-west (or the reverse in the southern hemisphere) for optimal sunlight.

■ Raise to a height that suits you and your crops.

■ Make them a maximum of 10ft (3m) long and a width that's a comfortable reach to avoid standing on soil.

**As well as being** dug into the soil, a thick layer of well-rotted organic matter can be spread over the surface to act as a mulch.

**A typical raised bed** is 6in (15cm) deep. If your crops need netting, leave long corner stakes as a ready-made frame.

## Growing under cover

In cooler climates, greenhouses extend the growing season in spring and fall and raise temperatures in summer, making it possible to obtain harvests from more tender crops.

Situate greenhouses to receive light throughout the day, and make sure the roof vents are equivalent to 15–20 percent of the floor area to moderate summer temperatures. Opening vents allows insect pollinators access to flowering plants, but hand pollination may still be necessary. Cold frames, mini greenhouses, and cloches (below) are also handy for raising seedlings, hardening off young plants, and protecting new transplants.

## Planting out

Transferring plants to their final growing position is a critical time. Harden them off if raised under cover (see p.11) and treat gently to prevent damage. Always water plants in pots before transplanting; adding liquid seaweed helps to reduce shock.

**How to plant** Dig a hole slightly larger than the rootball. Water the base of the hole if dry and sprinkle in mycorrhizal fungi to help increase the absorption area of the plant's roots. Ease the rootball from the pot, place in the hole at a depth so that the soil surface matches the level of the growing medium, then gently firm the soil around it. Water in well, add any supports required, and shelter with fleece until established.

**Before planting**, gently tease out the roots to help the plant establish.

## Aftercare

Ensuring that your crops are kept clean, warm, well fed, and watered can mean the difference between success and failure.

**Watering** Thoroughly soak soil around the base of plants (not the leaves) to encourage roots to grow down into the soil in search of moisture. If given a tiny bit, roots will stay near the surface and dry quickly. Watering during the evening in summer reduces evaporation.

**Feeding** Don't encourage soft growth with high-nitrogen feeds; use a balanced general fertilizer, seaweed tonic, or high-potassium tomato feed to encourage flowering and fruiting. Acid-loving plants like tea need a specialty feed.

**Weeding** Weeds compete for moisture, nutrients, and light, so keep crops weed-free. A thick mulch of 2–3in (5–7.5cm) of well-rotted organic matter or composted bark spread over moist, weed-free soil effectively suppresses them. Always remove weeds before they flower and set seed.

**Protection** Cold winds, frost, and scorching sunlight can all damage plants. Use horticultural fleece to cover and protect crops from frost. Thick mulches and cloches also provide frost protection, while high temperatures can be mitigated using shade from netting.

**Water generously** near the base of the stem to encourage root growth.

**Use a hoe** to remove weeds between plants, or a hand fork around stems.

## Growing in pots

Choose the largest pots possible and ensure root crops have enough depth to grow well. Plastic pots hold moisture better and can be dropped inside terracotta pots to improve their appearance. Always make sure there is a drainage hole at the base, and cover the hole with pieces of broken pots or large stones to stop the hole getting clogged with soil.

Use a mix of 80 percent loam-based to 20 percent multipurpose, which is easier to rewet if it dries out. Keep plants well-watered when in growth, and consider using an automatic irrigation system if you're busy or often away. Feed plants regularly and repot perennials or replace the top layer of potting medium in their pot annually to keep them growing strongly.

# Choose your crops

Wonderful as it would be to grow all these amazing crops at the same time, it is more practical to start with a few. The following pages pick out plants suited to particular growing conditions or ambitions.

## CROPS FOR POTS

If you have limited space, these plants will work particularly well in containers. Many edibles thrive in pots, given the proper care. Containers are a great way to keep tender crops portable, too, if they need to be brought under cover in cold weather.

**Sweetleaf** The leaves of this tender perennial are the source of the sugar substitute Stevia–*see p.180*.

**Turkish orange eggplant** A compact crop that makes a decorative pot plant with its glorious orange fruits–*see p.26*.

**Shiso** Attractive, cinnamon-scented Japanese herb with wrinkled burgundy or bright green foliage–*see p.54*.

**Tea** An evergreen, acid-loving shrub, tea plants are best grown in pots if your soil is alkaline–*see p.178*.

**Hyacinth beans** Where summers are cool, grow this purple-podded legume in large pots under cover–*see p.30*.

**Cape gooseberry** Heart-shaped leaves and fruit enclosed in papery lanterns make for an attractive pot specimen–*see p.198*.

### Also try
■ **Jicama** Large pots suit this vigorous Mexican vine, grown for its white-fleshed tubers–*see p.116*.

■ **Turmeric** A heat-loving Asian spice grown for its boldly flavored and colored rhizomes and large, attractive, edible leaves–*see p.166*.

■ **Finger lime** A citrus shrub native to Australia and best grown in containers to move outdoors in summer and back under cover in winter–*see p.188*.

# FAST-GROWING CROPS

Edibles that race from germination to harvest in just a few weeks are ideal if you can't wait to try your new crops. Choose from this selection for maximum productivity or where space is at a premium, or if you need vigorous climbers to rapidly clothe walls or fences.

**Garland daisy** The featherlike leaves of this easy-to-grow green have a strongly herbal taste–*see p.76.*

**Fenugreek** The aromatic leaves of this annual plant are quick to crop, and seeds can be harvested later–*see p.154.*

**Rat-tail radishes** Grown for their spicy, pointed pods, these radishes quickly grow over 3ft (1m) tall–*see p.56.*

**Red orach** Sow every few weeks as a cut-and-come-again salad crop, or let it grow tall for mature leaves–*see p.60.*

**Achocha** Vigorous vine producing prolific crops of pods with a taste of cucumber and sweet pepper–*see p.48.*

**Hardy passion fruit** A tough, rampant climber that drips with heavy crops of summer fruits–*see p.206.*

**Callaloo** Grown as a cut-and-come-again crop, baby leaves of callaloo can be ready to pick 3–4 weeks after sowing–*see p.80.*

### Also try

■ **Snake gourd** The cylindrical fruits of this squash are eaten like zucchini when young or can be allowed to reach great lengths–*see p.22.*

■ **Hyacinth beans** A vigorous climbing bean with pretty flowers and delicious purple pods–*see p.30.*

■ **Salsola** Also know as "saltwort," the slender, succulent leaves of this salt marsh plant are a sought-after delicacy in Italy and Japan, and grow well in alkaline soil–*see p.88.*

# SHADE-LOVING CROPS

Every garden has a shady corner, but there is no need to struggle to fill it. Plenty of the crops in this book are woodlanders in the wild, which thrive when given shelter from the heat of the sun.

**Wood sorrel** Dainty and elegant ground cover; the trefoil leaves of this spreading plant taste like sharp apples–*see p.158*.

**White alpine strawberry** For evergreen ground cover and a steady supply of tiny, sweet, white berries–*see p.212*.

**Sushi hosta** Shoots, leaves, and stems of hostas are all edible and are a favorite vegetable in Japan–*see p.70*.

**Oregon grape** The blue-colored berries borne in late summer by these evergreen shrubs make lovely preserves–*see p.210*.

**Chokeberry** Attractive shrubs bearing white flowers, deep purple berries, and rich fall color–*see p.204*.

**Japanese ginger** Cold-tolerant species of ginger grown for its tender stems and flower buds–*see p.174*.

**Fish mint** The heart-shaped leaves of this perennial have a unique, slightly fishy, orange-cilantro flavor–*see p.162*.

### Also try
■ **Ostrich ferns** Shade-lovers, these statuesque ferns produce fronds up to 3ft (1m) tall. As the fronds unfurl in spring, their coiled ends can be picked and eaten–*see p.68*.

■ **Fuchsia berry** Following their showy, ballerina flowers, all fuchsias bear plentiful, sweet-tasting berries, but make sure you choose a cultivar known for its fruits–*see p.196*.

# CROPS FOR SOGGY GROUND

Wet soil is not traditionally used in gardens to cultivate edible plants, but with this selection of crops, there is no reason why a pond margin or bog garden can't be productive as well as beautiful.

**Skirret** This ancient root vegetable has a taste reminiscent of parsnips and carrots with a hint of pepper–*see p.122*.

**Ostrich ferns** Happiest planted in shade by a pond, the tips of their unfurling fronds are a spring delicacy–*see p.68*.

**Camas** Long, slow cooking turns the bulbs of these blue-flowered perennials into an edible delicacy–*see p.96*.

**Chinese artichoke** Grown for its knobby tubers, this perennial also has attractive mintlike foliage–*see p.106*.

**Meadowsweet** This moisture-loving plant produces a foam of edible flowers with the flavor of almonds–*see p.182*.

**Water celery** True to its name, this ground cover perennial with celery-flavored leaves thrives in wet soil–*see p.164*.

**Wasabi** The roots of this slow-growing perennial are the source of the potent green paste served with sushi–*see p.170*.

### Also try

■ **Fish mint** A popular ornamental that flourishes in wet soils, few growers realize its leaves can be used as a herb in Asian cooking–*see p.162*.

■ **Taro** This tropical crop is grown for its sweet-potato-like corms and large, edible leaves, and loves to be kept wet at the roots–*see p.112*.

■ **Mashua** The spicy tubers of this South American crop need constant moisture to plump up–*see p.102*.

# CROPS FOR SMALL GARDENS

Compact growth can be helpful when space is limited, but tall and climbing plants also take up little soil space and add interesting vertical elements to a display.

**Honeyberry** The dusty-blue berries of this compact shrub are packed with vitamin C and antioxidants–*see p.194*.

**Dahlia yam** Yes, you read it right: the tubers of many dahlias have a deliciously nutty flavor–*see p.98*.

**Chilean guava** With fruits like strawberry and bubblegum, this petite, unfussy shrub deserves a spot in any garden–*see p.190*.

**Strawberry popcorn** A miniature maize variety that produces small cobs of red kernels for popping–*see p.148*.

**Spilanthes** The edible flowers of these bushy plants produce a pleasantly tingling sensation–*see p.50*.

**Daylilies** The buds, trumpetlike flowers, stems, shoots, and roots of this ornamental perennial are all edible–*see p.130*.

**Asparagus peas** Given support, this spreading plant takes up little space and bears tasty, winged pods–*see p.38*.

## Also try

■ **Chia** Upright, but not spreading, the tall blue flower spikes of chia will add height to a small garden, and are followed by a crop of superfood seeds–*see p.142*.

■ **Mashua** A real multipurpose plant, mashua is a bushy climber with pretty, gray-green leaves and bright flowers, all of which are edible, along with the crisp and spicy tubers–*see p.102*.

# DROUGHT-TOLERANT CROPS

Plants that can withstand dry periods and still produce a harvest are unusual, but some of these tough crops can do just that. This makes them ideal for gardens in dry climates or on lighter, free-draining soils.

**Goji berry** These hardy shrubs withstand wind, drought, and salt-laden air to produce prolific crops of berries–*see p.202*.

**Yacón** This towering plant, with crisp, pear-flavored tubers, survives drought better than most root crops–*see p.92*.

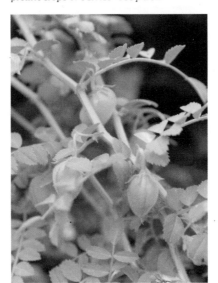

**Chickpeas** The roots of this legume probe deep into the soil in search of water, making it a less thirsty crop–*see p.34*.

**Amaranth** Varieties of amaranth grown mainly for their seeds crop better when watered sparingly–*see p.136*.

**Quinoa** This easy-care annual, grown for its protein-rich seeds, requires watering only in severe drought–*see p.140*.

**Huauzontle** Once established, huauzontle tolerates heat and drought to produce tender, broccolilike flower heads–*see p.86*.

**Strawberry spinach** A long taproot ensures good drought resistance and great yields of leaves and fruits–*see p.72*.

### Also try

■ **Earth chestnut** This pretty, white-flowered perennial needs almost no watering once established and produces tubers with a taste like chestnuts when cooked, leaves similar to parsley, and seeds like smoky cumin–*see p.118*.

■ **Sesame** The familiar burger-bun seeds come from a glorious flowering plant, similar to a foxglove, which needs high temperatures to thrive–*see p.146*.

# FRUITING VEGETABLES

**Level 2**
*moderate*

# Snake gourd

*Trichosanthes cucumerina var. anguina*

Squashes grow in a wide range of colors and sizes, and are known for the fantastic shapes of their fruits. Snake gourds are no exception, producing long, cylindrical fruits, which, left to their own devices, will coil up like a bed spring—or, as the name suggests, like a snake wrapped around a tree branch.

## What is it?

Snake gourds are fast-growing climbing vines believed to have originated in tropical Southeast Asia. The white, star-shaped flowers, with long, curly frills to the petal edges and a deliciously sweet fragrance, are rather small and delicate considering the supersized fruit that develop from them. Young fruits can be prepared and eaten in their entirety, like zucchini, while the red pulp of mature fruits makes a good substitute for tomatoes. Young shoots and leaves are also edible. Cooking removes the bitter taste that all parts of the plant have when raw. If you have kids (or even if you don't), keep a few mature specimens to paint and turn them into colorful vegetable snakes.

*To produce the longest, straightest gourds, some growers harness the power of gravity by tying weights to the ends of developing fruits.*

**Plants bear** both male and female flowers, and for fruits to form, male pollen must be transferred to female flowers.

## How do I grow it?

Given their tropical heritage, in cooler climates it pays to start plants off early under cover and plant them out in a warm, sunny spot in the garden. Snake gourds are vigorous climbers, so you will need to provide them with some sort of sturdy climbing frame to scramble over—a pergola is ideal. And, assuming you want to grow a few long, straight, mature specimens, whatever structure you choose should be at least 5ft (1.5m) tall, since the fruits will coil if they touch the ground.

**Fruits** of the longest varieties can extend up to 5ft (1.5m) but are best eaten when still under 18in (45cm) in length.

## Quick guide

**In cooler climates,** sow indoors in spring at 77-86°F (25-30°C)

**Some like it hot!** Minimum temperature needed for growth is 68°F (20°C)

**Grow in** a sheltered, sunny site outdoors in rich, moist, well-drained soil

**Keep moist** but avoid waterlogging

**Vines can** spread up to 16ft (5m)

**Harvest** long varieties at about 18in (45cm), smaller types at around 8in (20cm)

## Step-by-step growing »

# Step-by-step growing

To produce a good crop of fruits, snake gourds need warm conditions in a sheltered site, with free-draining soil rich in organic matter and regular watering throughout the growing season.

## When to grow and harvest

Start sowing indoors in spring and harvest the fruits when they are still young.

|  | early winter | late winter | early spring | late spring | early summer | late summer | early fall | late fall |
|---|---|---|---|---|---|---|---|---|
| sow indoors |  |  | ● | ● |  |  |  |  |
| plant out |  |  |  | ● | ● |  |  |  |
| harvest |  |  |  |  | ● | ● | ● |  |

## ① Sow indoors

In spring, sow seeds individually into 4in (9.5cm) pots filled with moist, all-purpose mix. Sow seeds vertically ¼in (5mm) deep. Keep in a propagator heated at 77–86°F (25–30°C) until they germinate, which should be within 2–3 weeks. When the first couple of leaves have appeared, transplant the seedlings into individual pots one size larger and grow on. Harden off the young plants once all danger of frost has passed (see p.62).

**Grow on seedlings** in fresh potting mix and place in a bright position.

## ② Plant out

Plant the young snake gourds at the same level as they were in their pots, and about 2ft (60cm) apart. Then form a raised circular ridge of soil about 3in (7.5cm) high, encircling the base of each plant. Always water within this circular area, so that moisture will soak down to the roots rather than draining away. Protect from early cold snaps with horticultural fleece or cloches, and feed a general fertilizer until they are growing well.

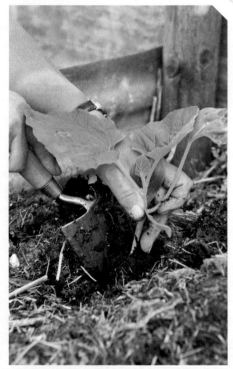

**Snake gourd** is a hungry crop and needs a rich soil to thrive.

2ft (60cm)

2ft (60cm)

**These vigorous plants** must be spaced far apart so they don't compete for water and nutrients.

## ❸ Train and prune

Provide a sturdy climbing frame for plants in the form of a strong trellis or pergola, or by building a large frame using stout canes or poles and covering it with netting; the structure should be at least 5ft (1.5m) tall. Train the stems up the vertical supports by tying them in regularly, and allow them to spread over the top.

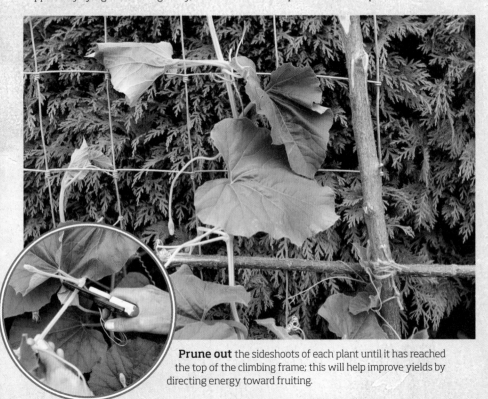

**Prune out** the sideshoots of each plant until it has reached the top of the climbing frame; this will help improve yields by directing energy toward fruiting.

## ④ Care and harvest

Once plants begin to flower, switch to a high-potassium feed. Pollination by insects can be erratic, and it may be better to cross-pollinate flowers by hand. Take a male flower and tap pollen from its anthers onto the receptive parts of female flowers, which have small, embryonic fruits at their base. Harvest long varieties once they reach 18in (45cm), and smaller types at about 8in (20cm).

---

### Cook's tips

#### Keep fresh
Keep young snake gourds in the refrigerator and use within a few days of harvesting. Larger fruits can be stored in a cool, dry place for several months.

#### How to eat
Young fruits can be steamed or sautéed like zucchini and substituted for them in recipes. Pick and eat only young fruits, as mature gourds develop a bitter taste.

- Slice finely and marinate with salt, sugar, white wine vinegar, and dill as a refreshing side.
- Chop and stir-fry with curry leaves and mustard seeds for a simple South Indian-style dish.
- Deep-fry snake gourd dipped in a chickpea flour batter and serve with a fresh cilantro or tamarind chutney.
- Chop the snake gourd into 2in (5cm) lengths, scoop out the center, and stuff with a mince or bean stew before baking.

#### How to preserve
Combine surplus fruits with runner beans in a dip, or slice, salt, and cover with sweetened and spiced vinegar to make a pickle.

{ Level 3
advanced }

# Turkish orange eggplant

*Solanum melongena x S. torvum*

This remarkable heirloom variety of eggplant is from a country that invented some of the finest eggplant dishes in the world. Perfect for growing in pots, the compact plants produce plentiful crops of sweet, well-flavored fruits with glossy, orange-and-green-striped skins that mature to pure orange and red.

## What is it?

Eggplants grow as perennial plants in warm regions and annuals in cooler climes. Some varieties form bushes as tall as 8ft (2.5m); the Turkish orange is a more modest variety, growing to a small but sturdy 24in (60cm). What it lacks in stature, it makes up for in productivity; bushes often end up heaving with fruits. The ancestry of eggplants is somewhat mysterious, but they may have originated in India, where wild forms are found.

*The eggplant is a member of the nightshade family of plants, which also includes tomatoes, potatoes, and capsicum (chili peppers, bell peppers, and paprika).*

**Flowers are "buzz pollinated,"** waiting for the correct wing frequency of visiting bees before releasing their pollen.

## How do I grow it?

Eggplants need a long growing season and prefer continuous warm weather throughout their lives, thriving in tropical and mid-temperate climates. In cooler areas, it is best to start seeds off under cover early in the year, keeping them at a steady temperature of 68–86°F (20–30°C). Continue growing plants under cover in medium-sized pots, a border in a greenhouse, or in growing bags; where outside temperatures are warm enough, you could even transplant into large pots and grow in a sunny, sheltered site. Pollination can sometimes be haphazard, especially if grown indoors, where the bees may not get at the flowers so easily. If this is a problem, you can take on the role of pollinator yourself by gently tapping the flowers or using a fine brush.

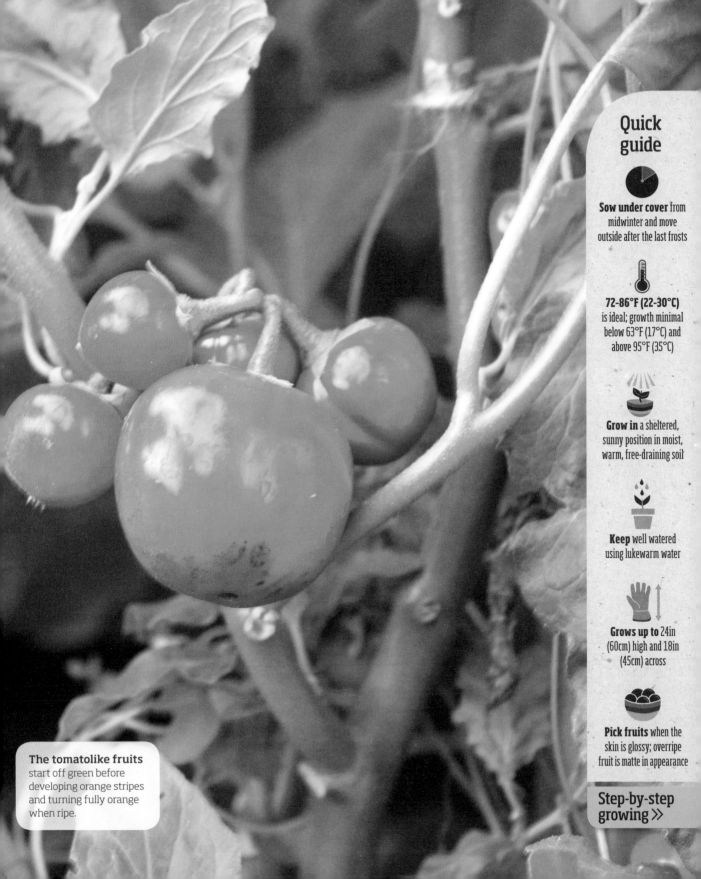

**The tomatolike fruits** start off green before developing orange stripes and turning fully orange when ripe.

## Quick guide

**Sow under cover** from midwinter and move outside after the last frosts

**72-86°F (22-30°C)** is ideal; growth minimal below 63°F (17°C) and above 95°F (35°C)

**Grow in** a sheltered, sunny position in moist, warm, free-draining soil

**Keep** well watered using lukewarm water

**Grows up to** 24in (60cm) high and 18in (45cm) across

**Pick fruits** when the skin is glossy; overripe fruit is matte in appearance

## Step-by-step growing »

# Step-by-step growing

Eggplants need warmth, sunshine, and regular feeding and watering to flourish. Most varieties only thrive outdoors in a hot climate and otherwise need the protection of growing under glass.

### When to grow and harvest
Late winter is the perfect time to begin sowing seeds and will give plants the longest possible growing season.

| | early winter | late winter | early spring | late spring | early summer | late summer | early fall | late fall |
|---|---|---|---|---|---|---|---|---|
| sow indoors | | ● | ● | | | | | |
| plant out | | | | ● | ● | | | |
| harvest | | | | | | ● | ● | |

## 1 Sow indoors

In late winter, around 8-10 weeks before the last frosts in your area, sow seeds in pots or modules of moist seed-starting mix on top of a refrigerator or dryer or in a propagator at around 64–70°F (18–21°C) and lightly cover. The temperature is important, as the seeds may not germinate if it is too low. Once the seedlings are large enough to handle, transplant them into larger pots, and then again if they start to outgrow those.

**Using a dibble** to pot up seedlings helps protect the roots from damage.

## 2 Plant

By late spring or early summer, the eggplant plants should be large enough to transfer to their final growing position. If you live in a warm climate, plant outdoors in a sheltered, sunny spot; otherwise, move them to a greenhouse border. Space plants around 20–24in (50–60cm) apart. If you are growing them in containers, plant them individually in 8–12in (20–30cm) pots of all-purpose mix.

**A warm, sheltered spot** is the most important requirement when growing eggplants.

20-24in
(50-60cm)

20-24in (50-60cm)

min. 8in (20cm)

**Grow in rows** 20–24in (50–60cm) apart, or individually in containers or growing bags.

## ❸ Aftercare

Stake and tie in the main stem as it grows. When plants reach around 12in (30cm) in height, pinch back or cut off the growing tip to encourage branching and fruiting. Feed with general fertilizer according to the manufacturer's instructions until established, then switch to tomato fertilizer once the first fruits have formed. Mist the foliage regularly with lukewarm water to discourage two-spotted mite. Water as soon as the soil surface starts to dry out. Allow access for pollinating insects if growing under cover. You can encourage fruit set by vibrating open flowers with your fingers.

**Stake and tie in** plants as they grow to keep them well supported.

## ❹ Thin out and harvest

Where you have a cluster of four or more fruits, it's worth removing one or two of the smaller fruits to help the others ripen and achieve a good size. Harvest fruits once they have turned a glossy red color. Compost plants at the end of the growing season.

{ Level 2 moderate }

# Hyacinth beans
*Lablab purpureus*

Hyacinth beans are great-value members of the pea family, with almost all parts of the plant edible and as much at home in the flower border as the vegetable patch. If you thought runner beans were vigorous, hyacinth beans easily outpace them, climbing up to 16ft (5m) in 3 months.

## What is it?

The hyacinth bean is a short-lived perennial climber that is usually grown as an annual in cooler climates, but can be overwintered for replanting the following year. The young pods are a popular vegetable in India—think purple sugar snaps—and the dry mature seeds are also cooked and eaten, or used for seed sprouts. In Africa, the leaves are harvested, too, and cooked like spinach. Purple pods rival the sweet pea-like flowers for attractiveness, particularly those of 'Ruby Moon' with their deep burgundy tones.

*Another name for the bean is "lablab," derived from the Arabic and thought to be an onomatopoeia for the rattle of seeds in the pods.*

**Hyacinth bean flowers** are self-pollinating, which means just a single plant will provide a good crop of beans.

## How do I grow it?

Originally from tropical India and China, hyacinth beans need warm temperatures to flourish. If the weather gets too cold, plants simply stop growing until conditions improve. In climates with cool winters and warm summers, extend the growing season by starting plants indoors, and repot them until soil and air temperatures rise enough for planting outside. Where summers are cool, grow under glass in fairly large pots and, provided you maintain a humid atmosphere to prevent pest problems, you can look forward to a good harvest. As climbing beans, they will need some sort of vertical structure to romp over; tripods of bamboo canes are the classic choice.

**The striking pods** retain their color if only briefly blanched in boiling water with a dash of lemon juice.

Step-by-step growing »

# Step-by-step growing

Hyacinth beans like warmth during germination. They will tolerate cooler conditions once established, but the best crops come from plants that have enjoyed consistent heat.

**When to grow and harvest**
Sow early for a long growing season and keep harvesting to encourage further flowering and cropping.

| | early winter | late winter | early spring | late spring | early summer | late summer | early autumn | late autumn |
|---|---|---|---|---|---|---|---|---|
| sow | | | ● | ● | | | | |
| plant out | | | | ● | ● | | | |
| harvest | | | | | ● | ● | ● | |

## ① Sow seeds

Soak seeds for 12 hours before sowing in small 3.5in (9cm) pots. Use moist potting mix and place two or three seeds in each pot, barely covering the seeds with potting mix. Place the pots on a windowsill or in a propagator at a temperature of 64–70°F (18–21°C). Thin out to leave only the strongest seedling.

Alternatively, if soil temperatures are warm enough, sow directly in their final growing spot (see step 3).

**Make multiple sowings** at regular intervals for a longer harvest.

## ② Harden off

Transplant seedlings into larger pots and continue growing at around 59°F (15°C) until outdoor temperatures warm sufficiently. So they don't suffer shock when planted outside, harden off young plants for 2 weeks by placing them outside during the day and bringing them back in at night; or move them to a cold frame and open and close the lid.

**Cold winds can damage** young plants, so place them in a sheltered spot when hardening off.

## ③ Plant out

Transfer plants to a warm, sheltered, sunny spot in moist, free-draining soil. Beans are hungry crops and it is worth enriching the soil by digging in well-rotted manure or growing medium. Set up climbing supports before planting and plant at the same depth as the potting mix in the pots.

6in (15cm)

6in (15cm)

**Space plants** at 6in (15cm) intervals and keep rows the same distance apart.

## Growing in containers

min. 12in (30cm)

Grow in pots at least 12in (30cm) in diameter, filled with organic potting mix with added loam-based mix. If growing in a greenhouse, mist the air around plants and damp down the path by pouring water on it 3 times a day, if possible, to discourage red spider mite.

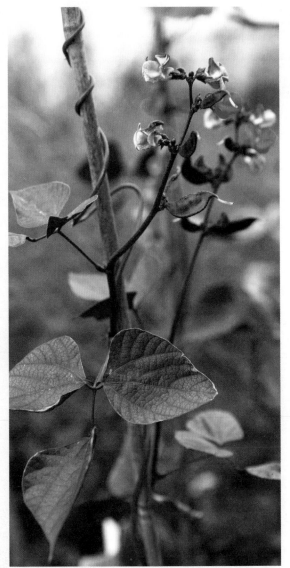

**Tendrils may need** tying in at first, but after that they will climb supports unaided.

## ④ Aftercare, harvest, and winter care

Keep plants weed-free and, once established, feed tomato fertilizer every 2 weeks. Water before the onset of dry weather to keep the flowers from dropping before they have had a chance to set. Harvest pods when they are still young and tender–no bigger than 4in (10cm) long–and pick continuously to encourage further flowering. Production will cease if pods are left unpicked, but if you have plants to spare it is worth leaving some to mature in order to harvest the seeds.

After fall frosts have cut down the foliage, lift plants out by the root balls with a garden fork, being careful not to damage the roots. Store in a pot or tray of old potting mix for protection, in a cool, frost-free location, such as a garage or shed, for replanting next year. Plants growing in warmer climates can remain outdoors year-round.

### Cook's tips

#### Keep fresh

Hyacinth beans do not store well: pick and eat the same day if possible.

#### How to eat

Prepare and eat young pods just as you would sugar snaps or green beans. Young leaves and shoots can be eaten, too.

- Lightly cook as a side vegetable: steam or boil for 1-3 minutes, or fry in a little oil with some chopped garlic.
- Add whole or sliced to stir-fries.
- For a quick-cook curry, make a tomato masala base, add the chopped beans with a little water, and simmer until tender.
- Mix raw or blanched into salads; they partner well with avocados.
- Slice and add to creamy pasta dishes: particularly good with pancetta or poached salmon.

#### How to preserve

Turn a glut of hyacinth beans into a bean chutney or piccalilli-style mustard pickle. Or leave excess pods to ripen fully, then shell and dry the mature seeds on trays in a cool, airy place.

## Quick guide

**Sow** under cover or direct at a minimum of 54°F (12°C)

**Minimum** 61°F (-16°C) to maximum 90°F (32°C)

**Grow** in well-drained soil and full sun; avoid growing in clay

**Drought-tolerant,** but water as peas begin to swell to improve productivity

**Plants grow** up to 20in (50cm) in height

**Pick** immature pods like "petit pois" or ripe peas when they are large enough to eat

**Level 2** moderate

# Chickpeas

*Cicer arietinum*

To grow fully mature, blond chickpeas, you need a long, hot growing season. But don't let that put you off, as an equally tasty harvest can be had by popping open young, fresh pods for their bright green, immature peas. You can even snip off a portion of young shoots and leaves to be enjoyed in salads.

## What is it?

Chickpeas are in the legume family of pod-forming plants that also includes peas, beans, and lentils. They produce relatively low-growing bushes with attractive, green foliage divided into paired leaflets, and bear flowers similar to those of a sweet pea. Like other legumes, they help improve soil fertility by taking nitrogen from the atmosphere through the action of bacteria that live in nodules in the roots. Because their root systems penetrate deep into the ground in search of water, they do not need vast amounts of watering for a successful crop.

*Up to three peas can be found in a pod, and each pea sports a small beaklike protuberance, from which they get the name "chickpea."*

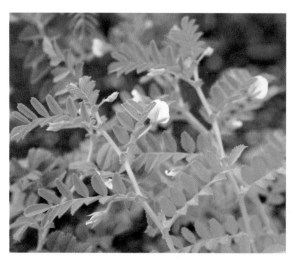

**Chickpea flowers** grow in varying shades of white, pink, purple, and blue, and usually start to bloom a couple of months after sowing.

## How do I grow it?

Seedlings sown early indoors should be ready to plant out in rows after around 31 days, but first need to be acclimatized to outdoor conditions. They can also be sown directly from midspring. The large seeds do not need a fine seedbed and are happy in most soils, apart from clay. Improve very poor soils with well-rotted organic matter, but not too much, as rich soil encourages leaves instead of flowers. Once growing, these drought-resistant, largely problem-free plants require little aftercare other than keeping down the competition from weeds.

**Chickpeas can** be picked when still green, and cooked and eaten whole like edamame.

Step-by-step growing »

# Step-by-step growing

Chickpeas are a low-maintenance crop; just keep them free of weeds and water when the pods are swelling, or if the young plants appear stressed, to optimize your crop.

### When to grow and harvest
Sow early indoors, as they need a long growing season, then sow directly outside when it's warmer.

| | early winter | late winter | early spring | late spring | early summer | late summer | early fall | late fall |
|---|---|---|---|---|---|---|---|---|
| sow indoors | | | • | • | • | | | |
| sow outdoors | | | | • | • | | | |
| plant out | | | | • | • | | | |
| harvest | | | | | | • | • | • |

 ## ① Sow indoors

Sow seeds indoors from early to midspring. Start by sprouting the seeds in a little water, then sow about 1½in (4cm) deep in root trainers or 3in (8cm) pots filled with seed-starting or all-purpose mix, one seed per pot or trainer. Water well with lukewarm water and place the pots on a sunny windowsill or in a propagator set to a temperature of 54–77°F (12–25°C). Germination will take 7–10 days. Once sprouted, transplant them before the roots become congested, as the seedlings dislike root disturbance. Alternatively, if soil temperatures are warm enough, sow directly into the soil (see step 2).

**Sprout chickpea seeds** before sowing by leaving them for a day or so in shallow water or dampened paper towels.

## ② Plant and sow outdoors

When the danger of frost has passed, harden off young plants for 2 weeks (see p.62) and, once acclimatized, plant them 2¾–6in (7–15cm) apart in rows 8–18in (20–45cm) from each other. Seeds can also be sown outdoors once the soil has warmed up, sowing directly into a level seedbed. Sow two seeds together, 2in (5cm) deep and 10in (25cm) apart. Water well until germination, then remove the weakest plant of each pair, leaving the stronger seedling to grow.

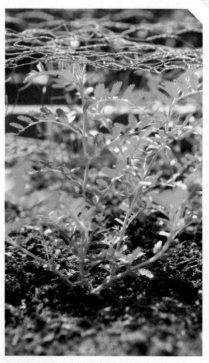

**Protect crops** from birds with chicken wire.

8–18in (20–45cm)

2¾–6in (7–15cm)

**Space plants** at the wider end of the range if growing in richer soil.

## ③ Aftercare

Once the young plants are established, chickpeas require little care other than weeding until a full leaf canopy has developed, which will then act as its own weed suppressant. Remove weeds by hand or use a hoe, taking care not to damage or accidentally uproot the developing plants.

Plants growing in nutrient-rich soils will often put on leaf growth at the expense of flowers, and therefore peas. If your soil is particularly rich, you can counteract this tendency by feeding plants a high-potassium fertilizer to encourage flowering.

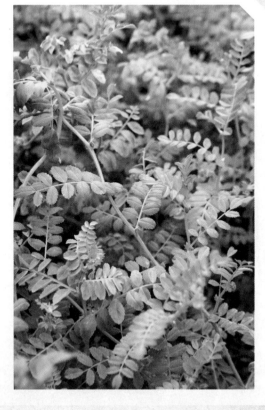

**Plants produce** a low, dense canopy of leaves that shades the ground and discourages weeds from growing.

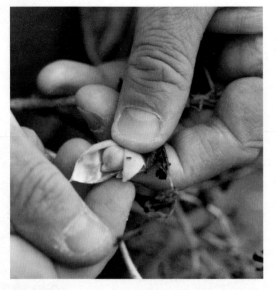

## ④ Harvest

Pick green pods regularly to encourage more cropping. Wear gloves to protect against the malic acid produced by leaves in hot weather, which gives them a red bloom and can be irritating to skin. Snap or snip them—either will do. If growing for the mature blond peas, harvest when the pods are dry, preferably on a sunny day, but don't leave them too long on the plant or rodents may get at them.

**After picking** the mature peas, leave them on a tray to dry, or use fresh.

---

### Cook's tips

#### Keep fresh
Store chickpeas loosely packed in plastic bags in the refrigerator and use them as quickly as possible.

#### How to eat
Chickpeas are versatile. Eat them fresh, dried, whole, puréed, mashed, or ground.

- Steam green chickpeas and briefly sauté with garlic and chili for a side dish.
- Sprinkle green chickpeas with smoked paprika and roast in the oven for a crunchy snack.
- Make a curry using chickpeas, Indian spices, kale, and grated fresh coconut.
- Combine cooked chickpeas with roughly chopped red onions, tomatoes, and parsley, then toss in a vinaigrette to make a delicious salad.
- Mix cooked chickpeas with Mexican spices, peppers, zucchini, and onions, then serve with tortillas, sour cream, guacamole, and lime wedges to make easy fajitas.

#### How to preserve
Cook until tender, cool, then dry. Once dried, refrigerate in a single layer in an airtight container for 3–4 days. You can freeze them for a year.

## Quick guide

**Sow indoors** from early spring or outdoors once risk of frost has passed

**Minimum** 46°F (8°C) to maximum 104°F (40°C)

**Grow** in an open, sheltered, sunny site

**Water** before the onset of drought, or as required

**Plants grow** up to 12in (30cm) high and 18in (45cm) across

**Harvest** midsummer to fall, when pods are 1in (2.5cm) long

*Level 2 moderate*

# Asparagus peas

*Lotus tetragonolobus*

If you love the taste of asparagus but don't have the time or space to grow it, this could be the perfect plant for you. While not the heaviest of croppers, what the asparagus pea lacks in volume it makes up for in the prettiness of its flowers and gourmet treat of its unusually finned pods.

## What is it?

Asparagus peas are wildflowers found in open fields in their native Mediterranean habitat, and are thought to have spread farther afield through imports of grain. Plants were first cultivated in gardens for their flowers, and it was only later that someone nibbled the pods and found they tasted delightfully like asparagus. Unlike many of their legume-family cousins, asparagus peas are trailing plants rather than climbers.

*The Latin name "tetragonolobus" means "with four wings" and refers to the arrangement of side fins on pods; when sliced they look like green stars.*

**The crimson flowers** resemble those of navy beans and are similarly attractive to bees. The central "keel" petals are darker than the upright "banner" petals.

## How do I grow it?

Seeds can be sown directly into the ground outdoors. As plants of the Mediterranean, however, they like warm soil to germinate and will need a little encouragement in cooler climates, either by first heating the soil with cloches or fleece, or by starting off seedlings under cover. Their attractive pealike flowers make asparagus peas excellent "dual-purpose" plants for a mixed productive-ornamental border, or as a low hedge around the vegetable garden. The plants have a rather lax habit, and if this isn't to your taste, try growing them through short pea sticks for support. If you pick pods regularly, plants will produce several harvests.

**Pods are at their best** when no larger than your thumb, and they should bend easily.

Step-by-step growing »

# Step-by-step growing

If plants are left unsupported, their spreading habit means you'll have few problems with weeds later in the season–they make productive ground cover under taller crops.

## When to grow and harvest

Sow indoors for early harvests because plants are not frost hardy. Pick regularly to prolong cropping.

| | early winter | late winter | early spring | late spring | early summer | late summer | early fall | late fall |
|---|---|---|---|---|---|---|---|---|
| sow indoors | | | • | • | | | | |
| sow outdoors | | | | • | • | | | |
| plant out | | | | • | • | | | |
| harvest | | | | | | • | • | • |

## 1 Sow indoors and plant out

In cooler climates or for earlier crops, sow seeds indoors at 66–70°F (19–21°C); germination can take up to 14 days. Sow in trays or 3in (7.5cm) pots of moist potting mix, two or three seeds to a pot, and thin to leave the strongest seedling. When 2in (5cm) tall, acclimate plants to outdoor conditions (see p.32, step 2) before transplanting to rows at final spacings (see step 2). Water with liquid seaweed to help plants establish themselves.

**Repot seedlings** started in trays once they outgrow the space.

## 2 Sow outdoors

Sow seeds outdoors once the danger of frost has passed. Drills should be ¾in (2cm) deep and 15in (38cm) apart. Thin seedlings to 8–12in (20–30cm) apart along the rows, once large enough to handle. In cooler climates, sow under cloches or fleece to help warm the soil.

15in (38cm)

8-12in (20-30cm)

**If you like** neat rows, support plants with pea sticks or using garden twine tied to canes at each end of a row.

## 3 Aftercare

Birds, especially pigeons, can strip plants of leaves, so protect with netting if likely to be a problem. Water in dry spells, particularly when flowering and as pods develop; keeping the soil moist also avoids problems with powdery mildew. Feeding is not usually needed, but a tomato fertilizer will encourage the production of flowers and pods in poor soils.

**Keep young plants** weed-free; they dislike competition when establishing.

## ④ Harvest

Pick pods regularly when they are 1in (2.5cm) long, checking your plants for the best-quality pods every day. It is worth doing so diligently as old pods become unpalatable, tough, and stringy. Harvesting is easier in the evening when the leaves close and pods are more visible.

**Picks pods** by pinching the ends between thumb and forefinger, or snip them off at the base with pruners or scissors.

## ⑤ Cut back

Plants can start to lose energy later in the season and look a little worse for wear. To help prolong their vigor, cut them down to 4-6in (10-15cm) from the ground, using pruners or garden shears, and this will usually stimulate a new flush of growth. Help them find their second wind by providing a few good soaks of liquid seaweed, and you should enjoy a sizable late harvest. When plants finally die back, snip them off at the ground but leave the roots in the soil so they release all the nitrogen they've been fixing.

### Cook's tips

#### Keep fresh

Best eaten as soon as possible after harvest, pods will keep in the vegetable drawer of the fridge for 2 to 3 days.

#### How to eat

Steam or lightly cook whole to preserve the subtle flavor, or slice finely into attractive crunchy "stars" that can be eaten raw.

- They are an excellent substitute for asparagus in most recipes, and perfect for fresh-flavored stir-fries, either sliced or whole.

- Steam whole and toss in melted butter with a dash of lemon juice and some shredded mint, then eat on toast.

- Slice and add raw to a new potato salad with capers and chopped boiled eggs.

- Stir into mac and cheese before baking, either on their own or partnered with ham hock.

#### How to preserve

The pods can be pickled in lime juice or white wine vinegar, though you'll find they lose some of their delicate flavor.

# SALAD VEGETABLES

**Cucamelons are** at their crunchy best when no more than ¾-1¼in (2-3cm) long.

**Level 1**
*easy*

# Cucamelons

*Melothria scabra*

Attractive and easy to grow, cucamelons pack the refreshing taste of cucumber with a zing of lime into one tiny, versatile fruit. They can be sliced and added to salads, pickled, cooked in stir-fries, dropped into cocktails, or blended into a cooling sorbet.

## What is it?

This ancient crop has been enjoyed in Mexico and Central America since pre-Colombian times, but only in recent years has the rest of the world started to discover its delights. Don't be deceived by the daintiness of the stems, leaves, and fruit: it's a tough, drought-tolerant plant, and avoids the usual cucumber pests and diseases. Somewhat slow to get started, it is usually trained upward, and will use its twining tendrils to climb and scramble rapidly up to 11½ft (3.5m). A single plant produces masses of fruit, so they are ideal for the smaller garden.

*Cucamelons are known as sandía de raton in Mexico, which means "watermelon for a mouse." Other monikers include "sour gherkin" and "pepquino."*

## How do I grow it?

Cucamelons love the heat and will put on rapid, vigorous growth in warm, humid conditions, so you may want to grow them under cover in cooler climates. Bearing in mind the vigor of plants, you will need to provide them with a trellis, or lightweight arbor or obelisk, over which to scramble. Alternatively, they can be grown up a wigwam of canes like runner beans. Cucamelons are suitable for growing in hanging baskets or raised pots, although when scrambling over the ground they are less productive. After first raising from seed, plants are more fruitful grown as perennials by lifting in fall and planting out again the following spring.

**Cucamelon seeds** need a warm, sunny windowsill or greenhouse propagator to germinate.

Step-by-step growing »

## Quick guide

**Sow under cover** from mid- to late spring and transplant outdoors after the last frosts

**Ideal temperature** for growing is 68-86°F (20-30°C)

**Grow in** a sheltered, sunny position, whether in pots or in the ground

**Plants will cope** with drought, but prefer plenty of water: check twice a day in the heat of summer

**Vines can** scramble up to 11½ft (3.5m)

**Pick grape-sized** fruits from midsummer to early fall; pick regularly for continuous cropping

# Step-by-step growing

Cucamelons are happiest in a warm, sunny position with plenty of room to scramble or climb. Although they are fairly resistant to drought, regular watering is rewarded with prolific cropping.

## When to grow and harvest

In cooler climates, the cropping season of cucamelons can be extended by starting plants off under cover.

| | early winter | late winter | early spring | late spring | early summer | late summer | early fall | late fall |
|---|---|---|---|---|---|---|---|---|
| sow indoors | | ● | ● | | | | | |
| sow outdoors | | | | ● | ● | | | |
| plant out | | | | ● | ● | | | |
| harvest | | | | | ● | ● | ● | |

## 1 Sow indoors

Sow seeds under cover from late winter to early spring in seed trays, small pots, or modules of seed-starting or all-purpose mix, making sure the seeds sit vertically in the medium. Place them on a warm windowsill or in a propagator at around 68-75°F (20-24°C), where they will take up to 4 weeks to germinate. Once two or three seed leaves have developed, lower the temperature to 64-70°F (18-21°C). When seedlings are large enough to handle, transplant into 3½in (9cm) pots.

**Transplant seedlings** to larger pots so they have space to grow.

## 2 Transplant

After the risk of frost has passed, either harden off plants to acclimatize them to cooler conditions (see p.62) and transplant them to a sunny, sheltered location outside, or move them to a border within a warm greenhouse or hoophouse. Space plants at 6-16in (15-40cm) if growing in a border. Cucamelons can also be grown in containers, with two plants to a growing bag or one per large pot. You will need to provide climbing support—trellis, nylon netting, or sheep fencing is ideal. If using cane supports, older canes or hazel poles can be easier for the tendrils to grasp.

**Tendrils find** the ragged edges of older canes easier to climb.

6-16in (15-40cm)

6-16in (15-40cm)

12-18in (30-45cm)

**Grow in rows** in a border, or plant individually in large pots, or have two plants to a growing bag.

**The climbing potential** of cucamelons must be tamed by pinching back and pruning to encourage fruiting.

## ③ Aftercare

The stems may need to be tied to supports until the plants are established, especially if growing up canes. Once the main shoots reach 8ft (2.5m), pinch them back at their growing tips, and trim sideshoots back when they reach 12–16in (30–40cm) long. This will encourage bushier growth and direct the plant's energy to forming flowers and fruits rather than leafy growth. Water regularly and feed a high-potassium liquid fertilizer if needed to boost cropping. Cucamelons are very resistant to pests and don't tend to be troubled by diseases either, making them particularly easy to care for.

### Cook's tips

**Keep fresh**

Store cucamelons in a plastic bag in the vegetable drawer of a refrigerator.

**How to eat**

Cucamelons can be eaten straight from the vine after washing and add a zesty freshness to salads, drinks, and preserves.

- Cut into halves or slice in salads or salsa.
- Toss simply with slices of peppers, olives, and a generous splash of olive oil.
- Use them in place of olives in a dry martini, or drop them into a gin and tonic or other gin-based drink.
- Turn excess into cucamelon dip or pickles (see below).
- Partner with lime to make an unusual jam.

**How to preserve**

Cucamelons are perfect for pickling. Mix them with white wine vinegar, sugar, salt, and a mixture of fresh herbs such as dill, mint, or cilantro. Boil until the sugar and salt dissolve, cool, and then refrigerate. The pickles will keep for 3–6 months in a sealed, sterile jar.

## ④ Harvest and winter care

Harvest begins after 2–3 months when the fruits are the size of small grapes. At the end of the growing season, but before the first frosts, lift the roots of plants and store them throughout the winter in a cool, frost-free place, covering the roots with coconut fiber or vermiculite and keeping them dry. Replant the roots the following year after the last frosts. Overwintered plants tend to crop earlier and more prolifically.

## Quick guide

**Sow** under cover and plant out once the danger of frost has passed

**Minimum** 46°F (8°C) to maximum 86°F (30°C)

**Grow** in rich soil in a warm, sheltered position in sun or part-shade

**Water** as required until established, depending on seasonal rainfall

**Plants grow** up to 10ft (3m) in both height and spread

**Harvest** continuously to encourage growth; pick young fruits and leave a few to mature

# Achocha

*Cyclanthera pedata*

**Level 2** moderate

This vigorous, easy-to-grow plant bears deep green, multilobed leaves and produces plump pods that taste of cucumber when soft and young, and sweet peppers when mature. Used as an anti-inflammatory, studies are also underway into its reputed ability to help lower cholesterol levels.

## What is it?

Achocha is an extremely rampant climbing, scrambling vine native to Central and South America. In its natural habitat, it grows at elevations of around 6,500ft (2,000m), where temperatures are cool but remain frost-free. So if you've always wanted to grow peppers but don't have a warm enough climate, achocha makes an excellent alternative. Young fruits can be eaten raw in salads or as a snack, while mature fruits can be cooked. The shoots and young leaves are edible, too.

### When to grow and harvest

Sow in spring for transplanting when the weather warms. Harvest through the summer and fall.

| | early winter | late winter | early spring | late spring | early summer | late summer | early fall | late fall |
|---|---|---|---|---|---|---|---|---|
| sow indoors | | | ● | ● | | | | |
| plant out | | | | ● | ● | | | |
| harvest | | | | | ● | ● | ● | |

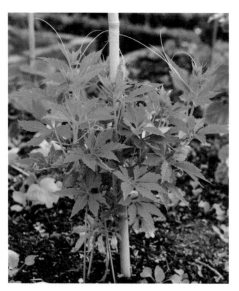

**If using bamboo canes** for climbing support, they are best inserted at the same time as planting to avoid damaging the roots.

## How do I grow it?

After sowing indoors, transplant outdoors, leaving it enough space to scramble over a trellis, frame, or netting. Pod production is best when the stems are supported, rather than grown over the ground. Grow in part-shade in hot climates to avoid sun scorch. Be warned: achocha is a rampant spreader and should only be grown under cover in areas with a short growing season.

###  1 Sow indoors

Start seeds off on a sunny windowsill or in a greenhouse. Sow in late spring in small pots filled with rich seed-starting mix, two seeds per pot. Place on a warm windowsill or in a propagator at around 68°F (20°C). Remove the weaker seedling after germination. When they look to be outgrowing their pots, transplant into larger ones.

## Cook's tips

### Keep fresh
Fruits keep well for 1 week in a cool, dry place.

### How to eat
Immature fruits can be eaten raw or pickled, but mature fruits are cooked. Leaves and young shoots can be eaten as cooked greens.

- Use as a substitute for cucumber in salads and dips.
- Fill with dill yogurt for a satisfying snack.
- Stuff with a rice or meat filling and bake in a tomato sauce.
- Make savory achocha jam.

### How to preserve
Cut the ends off immature fruits and pickle in vinegar with sugar or mixed spices.

## 2  Initial care

Harden off after the last frosts (see p.62) and plant out around 3ft (1m) apart to give each plant enough space to flourish. Protect the soft stems from drying winds with fleece or a windbreak until established. Train the stems up a support as soon as possible to avoid them becoming tangled. Mulch with well-rotted organic matter once established. Feed a general fertilizer, switching to a high-potassium feed when fruits begin to form.

## 3  Watering

Achocha needs copious watering. Raise a circular ridge of soil 2ft (60cm) away from the base of the stem and about 3in (7.5cm) high. Fill this every time you water so it will soak down to the roots rather than draining away. Burying a flowerpot near the base of the plant, or cutting the bottom from a plastic bottle and burying it nozzle-down, has a similar effect. Harvest regularly to encourage pod production. Save seeds for next year, then compost after the first frosts.

# Spilanthes

*Acmella oleracea*

**Level 1** easy

Thrill-seeking gardeners take note! The tight, yellow, cone-shaped flowers of the spilanthes look bonny in a border, but when eaten, their mild citrus flavor is followed by a strong tingling sensation, likened to popping candy, then numbing. The opportunities for creativity in the kitchen to surprise dinner guests are endless.

## What is it?

Spilanthes is a bushy, trailing plant, with lush foliage and plentiful chrome-yellow flowers. Native to the warm climates of the tropics, it probably originates from Brazil, where it is known as *jambu* and its leaves are used to flavor salads and stews. The unusual properties of its flowers have long been known and are still used medicinally in many countries to ease the pain of toothache, mouth ulcers, and sore throats, giving rise to another of its names: "toothache plant."

*The substance responsible for the flowers' electric effects also stimulates saliva production, so only sample a few at a time to avoid drooling.*

**Keep plants in containers** constantly moist and consider applying a ring of copper tape around the sides to deter adventurous climbing slugs.

## How do I grow it?

Spilanthes are perennial plants in their native environment, but they are not frost hardy and, in areas where temperatures dip below 32°F (5°C) in winter, they are usually grown outdoors as annual bedding. Plants are easy enough to raise from seed each year, however, or they can be lifted in fall and potted up for overwintering under cover, ready to plant out again next spring. The daisylike flowers make a great addition to an ornamental border, provided plants are given enough space to pursue their trailing habit. They are also suitable for growing in large containers, which has the added benefit of affording some height protection against slugs.

## Quick guide

**Sow** indoors from early spring or outdoors once risk of frost has passed

**Grow** in rich, moist soil in full sun or partial shade

**Minimum** 32°F (5°C) to maximum 95°F (35°C)

**Water** regularly and generously to avoid drought

**Plants grow** up to 16in (40cm) in height and spread

**Harvest** flowers and leaves from midsummer to fall

**Step-by-step growing ≫**

**The species bears** plain yellow flowers, or there is a variety with red florets in the center of the cone.

# Step-by-step growing

These fast-growing, tender plants are easy to grow as annuals given a rich soil that is kept moist. Their colorful flowers suit ornamental borders and containers, as well as kitchen gardens.

**When to grow and harvest**
Start sowing indoors to prolong the growing season and pick flowers frequently to encourage more buds.

| | early winter | late winter | early spring | late spring | early summer | late summer | early fall | late fall |
|---|---|---|---|---|---|---|---|---|
| sow indoors | | | ● | ● | | | | |
| sow outdoors | | | | | ● | ● | | |
| plant out | | | | | ● | ● | | |
| harvest | | | | | | ● | ● | ● | ● |

## ① Sow indoors

In cooler climates, sow seeds indoors at 68–75°F (20–24°C) on a warm windowsill, in a propagator, or in a greenhouse. Seeds need light to germinate and are best sown on the surface of trays of moist seed-starting mix. They should germinate in 7–14 days. Once seedlings are about 2in (5cm) tall, carefully prick them out and plant individually into 3in (7.5cm) pots filled with all-purpose mix. Continue to grow on under cover, repotting into larger pots if necessary.

**Use a dibble** to help prick out the tiny seedlings without damaging the roots.

## ② Plant out

Once the risk of frost has passed, acclimatize plants by hardening them off for a week or so (see p.62). Improve soil fertility and structure at the planting site by digging in plenty of well-rotted organic matter. Leave the soil to settle for a few days, then plant your daisies with 14in (35cm) between plants and rows.

Seeds can also be sown directly into prepared soil outdoors after the last frosts. It can be helpful in cooler climates to warm soil with fleece or cloches before sowing. Sow several seeds at 14in (35cm) intervals and thin to leave the strongest.

**Acclimatize young plants** for a week or so before planting out.

14in (35cm)

14in (35cm)

**Spilanthes** are trailing plants and need ample room to spread.

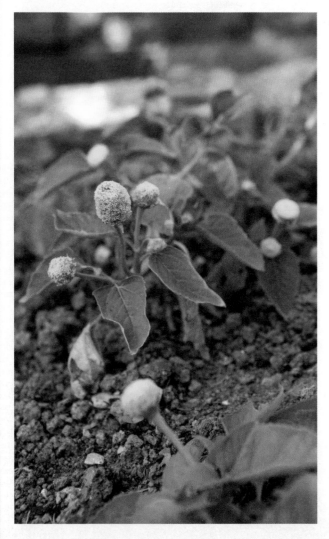

## ③ Aftercare and harvest

Once established, plants will grow rapidly. Water often during dry weather and feed a high-potassium tomato fertilizer to promote flowering. Pinch back growing tips regularly to create bushy plants and maximize flowering. Protect lush young growth from slugs and snails. There are a variety of environmentally friendly ways to do this, such as encouraging predators like beetles and toads, using nematodes, dousing with garlic spray, and luring into hollowed-out grapefruits.

The flowers, buds, and leaves can all be eaten and, once plants are established, can be picked as required.

**The electric effects** of the flowers are best enjoyed in small doses, which means just a few plants are normally enough for one household.

## ④ Winter care and propagation

Plants will be killed by frosts, but it is possible to overwinter them by lifting in late fall, potting up, and moving them into the house or heated greenhouse. Softwood cuttings taken during summer can be overwintered in the same way. To take a cutting, snip off a nonflowering shoot with two or three pairs of leaves and a 2in (5cm) stem. Remove the lowest pair of leaves and the soft tip of the shoot just above the growing point. Plant the cutting in a pot filled with moist cutting compost and place somewhere shady, ideally in a propagator.

## Cook's tips

### Keep fresh
Eat both leaves and flowers promptly after picking. They will keep for one or two days in the refrigerator.

### How to eat
This plant's potent tingling effect means it is normally used raw, in small quantities, as a garnish or spicelike addition to dishes.

- In Brazil, the leaves and flowers are sliced and mixed with chilies and garlic in a traditional condiment eaten with chicken or fish.
- Chop and add raw flowers to salads for a splash of color and peppy flavor.
- Liven up cocktails by stirring in small amounts of shredded flowers, or line the lip of a margarita glass.
- Cooked leaves have a more subtle flavor and make tasty leafy greens in spicy stews and soups.

### How to preserve
Flowers hung up to dry after picking, and carefully stored away from moisture and light, will continue to produce their characteristic zip for at least 1 year.

# Shiso

*Perilla frutescens var. crispa*

**Level 1** easy

If you like basil, then why not try growing shiso, its more spicy cousin with cinnamon-scented leaves? Popular in Japanese cuisine, shiso has soft, attractively wrinkled leaves in deep red and bright green varieties, which look impressive grown side-by-side in the herb garden.

## Quick guide

**Sow** under cover in early spring, or outdoors when the soil has warmed up

**Minimum** 30°F (-1°C) to maximum 86°F (30°C)

**Grow** in moist, light, free-draining, slightly acidic soil in a sunny or partially shady spot

**Water** regularly but avoid waterlogging

**Plants grow** up to 24in (60cm) in both height and spread

**Pick young**, tender leaves, growing tips, and flowers from late spring to fall

## What is it?

Shiso is native to China and is mentioned in ancient Chinese manuscripts. Brought to Japan in the 8th century, it was used in cooking and as a medicinal plant. In the West, shiso has mainly been grown for its ornamental foliage as a bedding plant, but more and more growers are discovering its culinary appeal. Both types are great in salads, as a wrap for sushi, or served with raw fish in sashimi; the green form is milder. The pretty, edible flowers can be used as a garnish, too.

### When to grow and harvest

Shiso is a fast-growing crop, so harvest regularly when the leaves are young and tender.

| | early winter | late winter | early spring | late spring | early summer | late summer | early fall | late fall |
|---|---|---|---|---|---|---|---|---|
| sow indoors | | ● | ● | | | | | |
| sow outdoors | | | | ● | ● | | | |
| plant out | | | | ● | ● | | | |
| harvest | | | | | ● | ● | ● | ● |

**Plants in containers** can be brought indoors before the first fall frosts and kept in a cool, bright place as houseplants over winter.

## How do I grow it?

Shiso is easy to grow but dislikes frost, so buy plants from the garden center after the last frost, or sow seeds in a heated propagator 8–12 weeks beforehand. Sow the seed fresh, as it rapidly loses the ability to germinate. Shiso can withstand drought but will give you a better harvest if you water it well. Grow it in window boxes by the kitchen for easy access.

### 1 Sow indoors

Sow under cover in seed trays for planting out after the last frost. Sow seeds on the surface of moist, well-drained seed-starting mix combined with sharp sand to improve drainage, at a ratio of 9:1. Press lightly into the soil and cover with a little potting mix, perlite, or vermiculite. Cover the tray with newspaper and place on a shady windowsill or in a propagator at 72°F (22°C). Germination takes 15–30 days. Once sprouted, uncover and place in the sun.

## ② Pot up seedlings

Once the seedlings are large enough, carefully transplant them into individual pots. Repot seedlings each time they outgrow their previous pot, but before the medium gets too congested with roots and they become pot-bound. The final pot should be no larger than 3½in (9cm), as smaller plants establish better than large ones.

## ③ Plant out

Once all risk of frost has passed, harden off the young plants for a week or so by placing them outdoors during the day and bringing them in at night, or keeping them in a cold frame with the lid ajar during the day. Once the plants are acclimatized and the weather has warmed up, plant them out in rows, 12in (30cm) apart with 12in (30cm) between each row. Protect them with horticultural fleece or cloches at first, removing these once the weather is consistently warm.

# Rat-tail radish

*Raphanus sativus var. caudatus*

{ Level 1 easy }

If you thought radishes were only about the roots, think again. While all radishes produce edible seed pods, the rat-tail radish doesn't focus on roots and instead puts most of its energy into producing a prolific number of spicy pods.

## What is it?

Also known as the serpent radish, the rat-tail radish is an exotic variety of the humble garden radish, thought originally to have come from the island of Java in Indonesia, and now popular throughout Southeast Asia. These annual plants can quickly grow to an impressive height, up to 5ft (1.5m) tall, bearing extensive, candelabra-like flowering stems from which the upright pods form. Pods are crunchy on the outside, juicy on the inside, and can extend to 12in (30cm) in length, but are best picked when still short and tender. The bee-friendly flowers are also edible and make a flavorful garnish, but don't pick them all or there'll be none to turn into pods.

> *Radish seed pods are a popular snack in Germany, where they are traditionally enjoyed with beer— hence the variety 'München Bier'.*

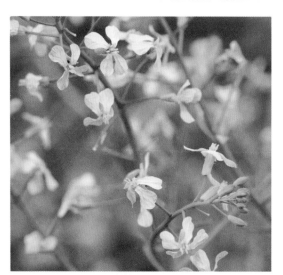

**The small, delicate flowers** can be pure white or tinged pink and will attract masses of pollinators into the garden.

## How do I grow it?

Rat-tail radishes are fast-growing, cool-weather plants that should still crop successfully sown early or late in the growing season. Sow direct and make repeat sowings as soon as the previous batch has germinated. Seeds can be sown in drills to form rows, or broadcast and thinned out to the correct spacing. Don't try growing plants too close together, as they resent overcrowding, and remove any encroaching weeds for the same reason. Keep well watered until they are established, and continue watering regularly after that to prevent the pods becoming tough. These tall-growing plants have relatively weak roots and will need staking to keep them upright.

Rat-tail pods are pale green in color, sometimes with pinkish markings, or there are purple-podded cultivars available.

## Quick guide

**Sow** in succession from early spring until midsummer

**Ideal range** 50-61°F (10-16°C); germination fails above 95°F (35°C)

**Grow** in sun to part-shade, where soil has been manured for the previous crop

**Keep** the soil constantly moist

**Plants grow** up to 5ft (1.5m) high and 2ft (60cm) across

**Pick** when still young and tender; older pods turn hard and bitter

**Step-by-step growing >>**

# Step-by-step growing

Rat-tail radishes need a constant supply of moisture to grow well, so plant them in deep, moisture-retentive soil, and give them plenty of room to grow. Plants are highly productive over a long period.

**When to grow and harvest**
Sow seeds under cover as early as late winter and outdoors until late summer to extend the cropping season.

| | early winter | late winter | early spring | late spring | early summer | late summer | early fall | late fall |
|---|---|---|---|---|---|---|---|---|
| sow indoors | | ● | ● | | | | | |
| sow outdoors | | | ● | ● | ● | ● | | |
| harvest | | | | | ● | ● | ● | ● |

## 1 Sow indoors

For an early harvest, begin sowing seeds under cover in late winter. Sow in modular trays, one seed per module—this will minimize root disturbance when the seedlings are lifted, whereas the roots of plants raised in trays can become intertwined, causing damage no matter how gently they are teased apart. Pot up seedlings in individual pots when they have outgrown their modules, and plant outdoors in early spring at the final spacings given in step 2.

**Heart-shaped seed leaves** appear first, before the true leaves come through.

## 2 Sow outdoors

Sow seeds directly outside from early spring. Seed drills should be ½in (1cm) deep and 12in (30cm) apart. Sow evenly along the rows and thin seedlings to 8in (20cm) apart, or alternatively sow three seeds every 8in (20cm) and thin to leave the strongest seedling. You can also broadcast sow by scattering seed over the entire growing area and then thinning to the correct spacing. You will need to thin the seedlings out several times before the correct spacing is reached.

**Thin out plants** progressively, leaving the largest and strongest in place.

12in (30cm)

8in (20cm)

**Avoid overcrowding** by spacing rows 12in (30cm) apart and leaving 8in (20cm) between plants.

## ③ Aftercare

Keep the soil moist, but don't overwater them. Cover the developing plants with fine netting or horticultural fleece to protect them from cabbage white butterflies and their caterpillars, as well as flea beetles. If canola is grown nearby and has recently been harvested, you may find pollen beetle infestations can delay or hinder cropping. Canola is in the same family as rat-tail radishes and, after the crop has been harvested, the beetles turn to the radishes as a new food source, feasting on the flower pollen and thereby preventing pods from forming.

**Each flowering stem** can grow over 3ft (1m) tall and will produce numerous pods, as long as pollination is not interrupted.

## ④ Harvest

Pick the pods regularly when they are small to prolong the cropping season. Cut off the pods with scissors or snap them off with your finger and thumb. When plants die back at the end of the season, simply dig them out and add them to the compost pile.

**Pods and plants** are easily damaged, so take care when harvesting.

### Cook's tips

#### Keep fresh
Wash pods and dry them thoroughly with paper towel before placing them in airtight bags. Avoid overfilling the bags. They will stay fresh in the vegetable drawer of the refrigerator for up to 1 week.

#### How to eat
Radish pods add a crunchy texture and peppery flavor to raw or cooked dishes.

- Add raw to salads, whole or sliced depending on size.
- Cook briefly in stir-fries.
- Lightly steam or blanch and enjoy as a side dish.
- Add to curries and stews in place of okra.

#### How to preserve
Pickling is the best way to preserve the crunch and spiciness of the pods. Pickle them in white vinegar with sprigs of lemon verbena leaves, or in cider vinegar flavored with smoked paprika. Leave for at least 1 month, or preferably longer, so that the pods have time to absorb the flavors.

## Quick guide

**Sow under cover** from early spring and outdoors from early summer

**Minimum** -22°F (-30°C) to maximum 95°F (35°C); leaves can scorch in hot sun

**Plant in** rich soil in a sunny or partly shaded position

**Water** freely for rapid growth

**Plants reach** up to 4ft (1.2m) and spread 12-24in (30-60cm)

**Pick leaves** as required throughout the growing season

# Red orach

**Level 1** easy

*Atriplex hortensis var. rubra*

Adding splashes of natural color can make any meal more exciting, and red orach leaves are some of the most vivid in the plant world. Add in some succulent young leaves to brighten up a salad, and lightly cook mature leaves for a salty, purple alternative to spinach.

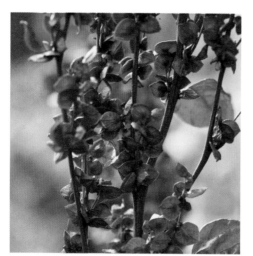

**Purple flowers** are borne on flowering spikes and take the form of hundreds of papery disks, each enclosing a single seed.

## What is it?

Red orach is a close relative of the common orach or spear saltbush (*Atriplex patula*), a plant now thought of as a garden weed but once considered a poor person's potherb. Red orach is the gourmet version, retaining all the vigor of a weed but with a far more refined flavor. Plants grow tall and stand firm at over 3ft (1m) in height, and with the stems, spear-shaped leaves, and flowering spikes all displaying a deep red-purple hue, orach's vibrant appearance stands out in the kitchen garden and would be a good choice for foliage color in a mixed or ornamental context. Plantings work especially well alongside low-growing pot marigolds (*Calendula*), whose edible orange flowers offer a striking color contrast, both in the garden and side-by-side in salads.

## How do I grow it?

Red orach is an annual that grows from seed each year, but this is the kind of plant you only need to buy once since it self-seeds so prolifically. In fact, it is highly advisable to pinch off the flower heads and collect the seed before it has ripened, or you and your garden risk becoming overwhelmed. Orach is fully hardy, but seeds need relative warmth to germinate, and for an early harvest it is best to start plants off under cover. Alternatively, sow directly outdoors once the soil has warmed up enough. For the largest, most succulent leaves, it pays to improve the soil with well-rotted organic matter.

*Orach was once more popular than spinach and, with high levels of vitamin C and immunity-boosting ascorbic acid, used as a remedy for sore throats.*

**Repeat-sow** for a supply of smaller leaves, or sow two main crops a year and allow them to mature.

Step-by-step growing ≫

# Step-by-step growing

Red orach is a hardy plant that can be harvested until late in the year. It needs a constant supply of moisture for optimum growth, so grow plants in moisture-retentive soil and water well in periods of drought.

### When to grow and harvest
Make early sowings under cover for an early harvest, then direct sowings outdoors.

| | early winter | late winter | early spring | late spring | early summer | late summer | early fall | late fall |
|---|---|---|---|---|---|---|---|---|
| sow indoors | | | • | • | | | | |
| plant out | | | | • | | | | |
| sow outdoors | | | | | • | • | • | • |
| harvest | | | | • | • | • | • | • |

## 1 Sow under cover

For an early crop, start sowing seeds under cover in early spring and you will have leaves ready to harvest by late spring. Sow seeds into modular trays filled with moistened seed-starting mix and lightly cover the seeds with perlite (an inorganic medium additive) or fine layer of potting mix. Germination will take 7–10 days. Once sprouted, keep the seedlings well-watered and transplant them to larger individual pots when they look to be outgrowing their modules.

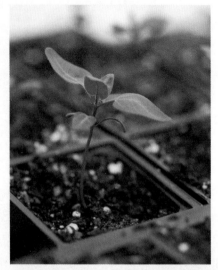

**Sow one seed** per module and gently push out both seedling and medium to pot up.

## 2 Harden off

Once all risk of frost has passed, harden off the young plants for a week or so by placing them outdoors during the day and returning them to shelter at night. Alternatively, transfer the plants to a cold frame, if you have one (it's a wooden box hinged at one end, with a tilted glass lid), and prop the lid open during the day before shutting it again at night. This allows the plants to become gradually accustomed to a harsher, more changeable environment.

**Start hardening off** on a mild day, gradually increasing the plants' exposure to colder temperatures, wind, and rain.

## 3 Transplant

Red orach can scorch in strong sunlight and is best grown in partial shade, or where plants will benefit from the shade of taller vegetables. Rich soil produces large, succulent leaves, so dig in plenty of well-rotted organic matter, if needed, before transplanting at the spacings shown in step 4.

## 4 Sow direct

Make further sowings directly outdoors to prolong the harvest. Sow every 2–3 weeks for a continuous supply of cut-and-come-again salad leaves, or for mature leaves, sow a second crop in midsummer. Rake the soil to a fine tilth before sowing thinly in rows ½in (12mm) deep and 24in (60cm) apart. Cover lightly with soil and water with a fine rose on the watering can. Thin seedlings to 10in (25cm) apart.

24in (60cm)

10in (25cm)

**Leave 10in (25cm)** between seedlings and transplanted plants, in rows 24in (60cm) apart.

## 5 Aftercare

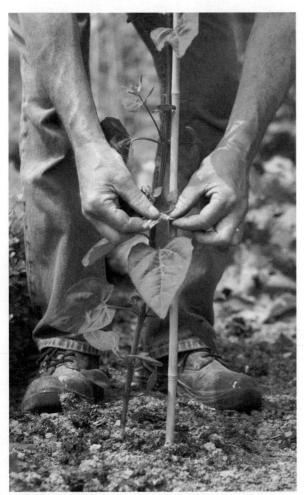

**Tall, leggy plants** may need to be supported by tying them to bamboo canes with garden twine.

Cover seedlings and young plants with netting to protect them from bird attacks. Hoe regularly between rows to remove any weeds and keep the soil moist. Avoid splashing leaves if watering in sunshine, which can scorch them; watering in the evening is more effective and avoids the problem. Start harvesting the young leaves when the plant is around 4–6in (10–15cm) tall, leaving the mature leaves on the plant. For bushier growth, you can "pinch back" the main stems and sideshoots by using your thumb and finger to remove the growing tips.

*Cook's tips*

### Keep fresh

Leaves are best eaten freshly harvested, though they will store for 2–3 days in a plastic bag in the vegetable drawer of the refrigerator.

### How to eat

Young leaves can be used in any recipe that calls for salad leaves, either on their own or to add a splash of color, while mature leaves substitute well for spinach.

- Partner with beets, goat cheese, and orange slices for a tangy salad.
- Use larger mature leaves to make brightly colored dolmades; try including beans and artichoke hearts in the filling mix.
- Make a nutritious cream of red orach soup.
- Stir at the last moment into pasta dishes; the taste of orach suits both tomato- and cream-based sauces.

### How to preserve

To freeze an abundance of leaves, blanch in boiling water for 1 minute and leave to cool before squeezing out excess water and transferring to a plastic bag.

{ } **Level 1** easy

# Society garlic

*Tulbaghia violacea*

Society garlic is so called because, though it tastes similar to garlic, eating it doesn't cause bad breath, so you can chomp away on the leaves, stems, buds, and flowers with no fear of social offense. The flavor is actually more similar to wild garlic with a hint of pickled onion.

## What is it?

This plant is from the African branch of the onion family and is more usually planted for ornamental bedding. Growing from rhizomes, plants produce neat clumps of flat, narrow leaves and bear clusters of fragrant, pale purple flowers on tall, slender stems. The flowering season is long, lasting from midspring to early fall, and though blooms are few at the start of the season, numbers gradually increase toward the end.

### When to grow and harvest

Harvest leaves as required throughout the growing season and pick flowers and stems as they appear from midsummer.

|  | early winter | late winter | early spring | late spring | early summer | late summer | early fall | late fall |
|---|---|---|---|---|---|---|---|---|
| plant |  |  | • | • | • | • | • |  |
| harvest |  |  | • | • | • | • | • | • |

**Society garlic** works well in containers, as it is relatively drought tolerant and the flowers make it an attractive addition to a patio or balcony.

## How do I grow it?

Tulbaghias make excellent plants for patio containers and are ideal for small gardens. Though not frost hardy, they will thrive in terracotta pots with a free-draining potting mix, and can be stored indoors in a cool, frost-free place over winter. They will also do well in a gravel garden, where the layer of gravel not only provides protection from light frosts in winter, but also stops them drying out too much in summer.

## ① Plant out or in pots

Grow plants in a sheltered position in warm sunshine, in well-drained soil or, if planting in pots, gritty potting mix. Plant out container-raised plants anytime from spring until fall. Water the plants and allow to drain. Dig a hole slightly larger than the pot they are growing in and at the same depth. Water the base of the hole if the soil is dry and ease the plant carefully out of the pot, planting it at the same depth as it was in the pot.

## ② Aftercare and harvest

Plants in the ground need only occasional watering in dry conditions to maintain production of foliage and flowers. Water plants in containers every few days. Feed all plants with a high-potassium plant food monthly, from midspring until early fall. Pests and diseases are rarely a problem. Harvest leaves near the base to keep the plant looking neat. Picking leaves, buds, and flowers will encourage the plant to produce even more.

## ③ Winter care

Cut back stems to 1¼in (3cm) above the ground in late fall. Society garlic doesn't tolerate cold conditions, so if you live in a cold area, protect plants over winter with a 2½in (6cm) mulch of well-rotted growing medium. If you have planted them in a gravel garden, then use straw or conifer clippings. Remove the mulch in spring when growth starts and the weather improves. Bring pot plants under cover.

# LEAFY
# GREENS

## Quick guide

**Plant** anytime from early spring to early fall

**Minimum** -33°F (-36°C) to maximum 68°F (20°C)

**Grow** in damp to wet, loamy, neutral to acidic soil in full or partial shade

**Water regularly** to keep the soil constantly moist

**Plants grow** up to 3ft (1m) in height and can spread to 18in (45cm)

**Pick** when new fronds are just breaking through in spring and are still small and tightly curled

# Ostrich ferns

**Level 1** *easy*

*Matteuccia struthiopteris*

Do you have a dark, damp spot in your garden and don't know what to grow there? Plant a few of these shade-loving ferns and you'll be rewarded with an exquisitely beautiful green vegetable ready for picking in early spring when little else is available.

## What is it?

*Matteuccia struthiopteris* is a deciduous fern, named for its resemblance to ostrich feathers. Its impressively large, bright green, infertile fronds emerge tightly coiled each spring from the crown, or rootstock, of the plant, and slowly unfurl. The coiled ends of these fronds are harvested for eating and have a refined flavor between asparagus and green beans. Shorter, brownish fertile fronds appear later.

### When to grow and harvest
The best time to harvest the tips is from early spring, before they unfurl.

| | early winter | late winter | early spring | late spring | early summer | late summer | early fall | late fall |
|---|---|---|---|---|---|---|---|---|
| plant | | | • | • | • | • | • | |
| harvest | | | • | • | | | | |

## How do I grow it?

Ostrich ferns dislike hot, dry summers and are perfect for growing outdoors in temperate regions. They look great planted in naturalistic groups and are happiest in a shaded area by a pond, but any sheltered, damp spot will do. Ostrich ferns spread by underground stems, and it is not uncommon to discover new plants suddenly popping up quite a distance from the parent. They are best grown from young container-raised plants bought at a nursery or garden center.

### 1 Plant out

Thoroughly water the container-raised plants and allow to drain. Dig a hole slightly wider than their current pot, but at the same depth. Water the base of the hole if the soil is dry and allow it to soak away, then scatter a root-booster of mycorrhizal fungi over the base. Ease the fern gently from the pot, teasing out the roots, and position it in the hole. Firm the soil around the root ball to remove air pockets, and give it a good soak of water.

**Plant ostrich ferns** for the double benefit of an attractive plant and repeated cropping.

### Keep fresh

Wash the shoots and store in a plastic bag in the refrigerator for up to 3 days.

### How to eat

Before cooking, always remove the sharp-tasting fuzz that grows on the fern.

- Sauté with garlic and butter.
- Roast with lemon and capers tossed in oil.
- Add to a potato salad niçoise in place of green beans.
- Fry and use with Taleggio cheese as a topping for pizzas.

### How to preserve

Rinse, then blanch for up to 4 minutes. Plunge in cold running water for 3 minutes, then dry. Freeze for up to 9 months.

## 2 Aftercare and harvest

Mulch around the plants with a 2–3in (5–7.5cm) layer of well-rotted growing medium to trap moisture. Ferns don't generally need feeding, but if plants are lacking vigor, apply a general-purpose plant food when they have just started into growth in spring. Let the ferns grow for a few years before harvesting, and harvest only up to half the frond, or the plants will not survive. Cut with scissors 1–3in (3–5cm) down the stem from the rolled fronds.

min. 16in (40cm)

## Growing in containers

Grow individually in pots at least 16in (40cm) in diameter, in a mix of three parts all-purpose mix, one part sharp sand, and one part long-term potting mix. Feed a general fertilizer during the growing season and keep the potting mix moist.

# Sushi hosta

{ Level 1 easy }

*Hosta 'Sagae' and various species*

Now's your chance to beat the slugs and snails at their own game and eat your hostas before they do. Try the tasty young shoots, stems, and leaves as a springtime delicacy in salads, stir-fries, sushi, or tempura. The edible flowers look pretty as a garnish, too.

## Quick guide

**Plant** young plants in early spring or fall

**Minimum** -40°F (-40°C) to maximum 77°F (25°C)

**Grow** in a light to moderately shady spot in moisture-retentive, fertile soil or mix

**Water frequently**; never let the soil dry out

**Plants grow** up to 3ft (1m) with a spread of up to 20in (50cm)

**Pick** shoots early in the morning, before they unfurl

## What is it?

Hostas have been gathered from the wild for centuries in China and Japan, and are still popular in Japan where they are now grown commercially. Hostas are extremely hardy, shade-loving perennial plants normally grown in the ornamental border for their large, attractive, textured leaves. All hostas can be eaten, though traditionally the large-leaved species *Hosta montana* and *H. sieboldii*, and cultivar 'Sagae', are the plants of choice.

### When to grow and harvest

Plant in spring or fall and start harvesting when new shoots appear the following spring.

|  | early winter | late winter | early spring | late spring | early summer | late summer | early fall | late fall |
|---|---|---|---|---|---|---|---|---|
| plant |  |  | • | • |  |  | • | • |
| harvest |  |  | • | • |  |  |  |  |

**Planting in spring** allows a full growing season for the hostas to establish themselves before you start to harvest the following year.

## How do I grow it?

Hostas thrive in rich, damp soil and need plenty of moisture. All prefer a shady spot, though the tougher, large-leaved varieties can tolerate some heat; just avoid planting them in scorching sunshine. Hostas are great in small gardens, as they do extremely well in containers, provided they are kept constantly moist and not left to outgrow their pots: when the existing container is full of roots, split them up and repot them.

### 1 Plant

Improve the soil with organic matter and leave to settle. Water the plant and allow the container to drain. Dig a hole slightly larger than the container and water the bottom. Once the water has drained away, scatter mycorrhizal fungi around the base of the hole where they will come into contact with the roots. Tease out the roots and plant the hosta so the medium surface is just below the level of the soil. Water thoroughly and mulch.

## ❷ Protect from slugs

If slugs and snails are a problem, consider growing them in pots where they are harder to access. There are numerous ways to provide protection: use environmentally friendly nematodes; encourage predators like ground beetles, frogs, toads, and thrushes; collect them by laying a sheet of burlap or plastic on the ground, or an upturned, hollowed-out grapefruit, then dispose of by hand; place copper tape round pots; or douse plants with garlic spray.

## ❸ Aftercare and harvest

Keep plants well-watered during the growing season. Feed them a slow-release general fertilizer in spring to boost growth, but take care not to overfeed. When harvesting, take a few shoots from several plants rather than many from one plant, to encourage further growth. Remove and compost the leaves after they die back in the fall.

## Quick guide

**Sow** indoors from late winter, outdoors from midspring; fall sowings possible

**Minimum** -4°F (-20°C) to 104°F (40°C) or higher

**Grow in** full sun to part-shade, and keep crops weed-free

**Water well,** but they should survive a short dry spell

**Grows up to** 24in (60cm) tall with a spread of 18-24in (45-60cm)

**Harvest** young leaves for salads; pick berries when deep red and very ripe

{ **Level 1** easy }

# Strawberry spinach

*Chenopodium capitatum*

You'd struggle to find a more "yin-yang" plant than strawberry spinach, which somehow combines a leafy green with a berry-bearing fruit bush in one quirky, eye-catching crop. Enjoy the young leaves raw in salads or lightly cooked, then stick around for the sweet delights of ripe red berries.

**Tiny embryo fruits** form at the leaf joints of the flowering stems. They are pale green at first, before taking on a pinkish tinge, then swelling to deep red.

### What is it?

Native to the northern US and Canada, strawberry spinach is a hardy annual plant in the same family as beets and the edible weed lamb's quarters. This helps explain why the roots, which are also edible, have a hint of beets, and why you need to be careful not to mistake the seedlings for weeds. Plants form a low rosette of spear-shaped leaves with serrated edges, before sending out long flowering stems that form fruits along their entire length–which accounts for another of their common names: "strawberry sticks."

### How do I grow it?

For the earliest crops, sow under cover from late winter, but take care to acclimatize the young plants to cooler conditions before planting out. Alternatively, direct-sow after the last frosts, but be warned: germination outdoors can be erratic and take several weeks if the soil is not warm enough, so don't give up. Plants form a long tap root that makes them more heat-tolerant and drought-resistant than spinach, but for the most tender leaves and juiciest berries, it is better to keep the soil constantly moist.

*The plant has spread around the world from North America, reaching Europe in the 1600s through exports of wool and birdseed.*

**The "strawberries"** look much more like mulberries and are similarly composed of many small fruitlets.

Step-by-step growing ≫

# Step-by-step growing

Strawberry spinach requires an open site on warm soil. Plants can be slow to get going if sown directly outdoors, and for the best chance of a bumper crop, it pays to start seedlings off under cover.

## When to grow and harvest

Sow indoors from late winter. Harvest young leaves from early summer and pick fruits when very ripe.

| | early winter | late winter | early spring | late spring | early summer | late summer | early fall | late fall |
|---|---|---|---|---|---|---|---|---|
| sow indoors | | ● | ● | ● | ● | | | |
| transplant | | | | ● | ● | | | |
| sow outdoors | | | | ● | ● | | | |
| harvest | | | | | ● | ● | ● | |

## 1 Sow indoors

For early crops, sow seeds under cover from late winter to early summer. Sow in pots, modules, or trays of seed-starting mix, and cover the seeds with a light sprinkling of potting mix or vermiculite. Place in plastic bags on a sunny windowsill or heated propagator set to 59–68°F (15–20°C), and keep the potting mix moist. Germination should take around two weeks. When seedlings are large enough to handle, carefully transfer them to individual pots.

**Grow on seedlings** in cooler conditions but still under cover.

## 2 Transplant outdoors

Young plants should ideally still be quite small when planted out to minimize root disturbance, but don't rush it, as a frosty cold snap could kill them off. Acclimatize plants to outdoor conditions by placing them in a cloche or cold frame and gradually increasing ventilation, first during the day and then also at night. Carefully transplant them into their final positions at the spacings shown below.

**Firm in the soil** after planting and give the transplants a good soaking of water.

18in (45cm)

10in (25cm)

**Plant in rows** 18in (45cm) apart and leave 10in (25cm) between plants.

# ③ Sow outdoors

Strawberry spinach can also be sown directly outdoors, although germination can be slower if the soil has not warmed up enough and several sowings may be needed. Outdoor-sown seedlings also tend to grow more slowly at first. Sow seeds thinly in drills ½in (1cm) deep and 18in (45cm) apart, or scatter seed evenly over the seedbed and lightly rake in. Thin seedlings to 10in (25cm) apart when they are large enough to handle.

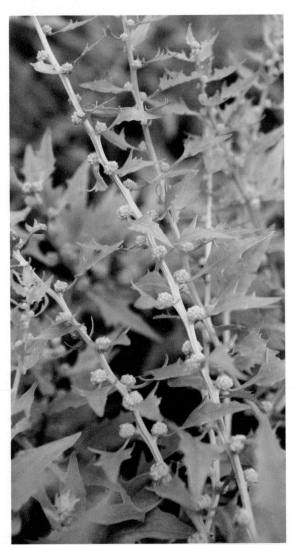

**Berries are green at first** and develop their rich red coloring as they ripen.

# ④ Aftercare and harvest

After transplanting, feed young plants liquid seaweed until they are well established and remove any weeds that will otherwise compete for moisture and nutrients. Plants can tolerate a degree of drought, but it is best to keep the soil moist. Harvest a few leaves from several plants rather than stripping a large number from a single plant, which will then take time to recover. Berries are sweet enough to harvest when they are deep red and very ripe. Strawberry spinach is a prolific self-seeder, and if you want to control seedling numbers, it is best to remove all the fruits before they fall to the ground.

## Cook's tips

### Keep fresh

Both leaves and berries will keep for 1 week in the refrigerator. Place the leaves in a plastic bag and store the berries in a plastic container.

### How to eat

The leaves can be used in place of conventional spinach in recipes. Young leaves are tender enough to be eaten raw, while mature leaves are better lightly cooked. The berries taste like nutty mulberries.

- Sauté the leaves with butter, garlic, and green beans for a tasty side dish.
- Top your breakfast muesli with a few berries for a sweet, musky flavor.
- Mix young leaves and berries with roasted baby beets and goat cheese for a hearty, fruity salad.
- Try cooked leaves and berries as a topping for pizza with blue cheese.

### How to preserve

Briefly blanch, then quickly cool and dry the leaves before freezing. Berries are best eaten fresh but can be used to make a jewel-like jam with bite.

**Cut leaves regularly** and remove flowers; stems will resprout fresh growth from the base.

# Garland daisy

*Level 1 easy*

*Chrysanthemum coronarium*

If you thought garland daisies were only good for cut flowers, think again. Also known as shungiku, the succulent leaves of this plant possess a sweetly herbal flavor and are robust enough to hold their shape well when added to stir-fries and stews.

## What is it?

Originally from the Mediterranean, *Chrysanthemum coronarium* is now well established as an edible crop in China, Japan, and Vietnam, where it is grown almost exclusively for its leaves. In fact, the process of producing flowers causes a chemical change in the plant that turns the leaves tough and bitter. That said, however, it is still worth letting a few plants run to seed since the attractive, daisylike flowers are themselves edible, and with even greater pungency than the leaves, a few scattered petals go a long way.

Look out for varieties described as having small or large leaves; the smaller-leaved types tend to have a stronger flavor.

**Plants will grow** quickly in a sunny position, but a degree of shade helps keep them cool in summer.

## How do I grow it?

Garland daisies make a neat edging plant for the border or vegetable garden, and will also do well in containers for the patio or balcony. As fast-growing annual plants that can withstand a light frost, they are grown easily from seed–leaves can be ready to harvest just 6 weeks after sowing–and are ideal for climates with cooler summers, or for early and late sowings in spring and fall. Plants actively dislike high temperatures, which can prompt them to produce flowers early, and it is best to avoid sowing seeds in spells of hot weather.

## Quick guide

**Sow outdoors** every few weeks from spring until 10 weeks before fall frosts

**Minimum** 39°F (4°C) to maximum 77°F (25°C), above which leaves turn bitter

**Grow in** sun or part-shade on any type of soil; growth is more tender in richer soils

**Keep plants** well-watered

**Can reach** up to 20in (50cm) in both height and spread

**Harvest** the topmost shoots when about 8in (20cm) long

**Step-by-step growing** »

# Step-by-step growing

Garland daisies are straightforward to grow, and the secrets of success are simple: sow regularly, don't neglect the weeding, water regularly, and harvest often for tender leaves with the finest flavor.

### When to grow and harvest
Garland daisies are productive over a long season, but keep harvesting to encourage young regrowth.

| | early winter | late winter | early spring | late spring | early summer | late summer | early fall | late fall |
|---|---|---|---|---|---|---|---|---|
| sow indoors | | • | • | | | | | |
| sow outdoors | | | • | • | • | • | • | |
| harvest | | | | • | • | • | • | • |

## ① Sow seeds

For an early crop, sow seeds in modular trays under cover from late winter. Once all danger of frost has passed, harden off the seedlings (see p.62) to acclimatize them to outdoor conditions, then transplant into their final positions at the spacings indicated in step 2.

Once the weather is reliably frost-free, sow seeds outdoors in drills or broadcast into a finely raked seedbed. To maintain a constant supply, sow every 3 weeks, sowing some in a sunny position and others in part-shade; seeds in sunshine will germinate and grow faster than those in shade.

**Seeds can be sown** in succession from late spring to early fall.

## ② Thin out and protect

Thin outdoor-sown seedlings to 4in (10cm) apart. Thin successively to achieve the correct final spacing, always removing the weaker-looking seedlings. But don't let these weaklings go to waste: enjoy the thinned seedlings in salads or as a microgreen garnish. If the weather becomes unexpectedly cool early in the season, protect the seedbed or young growth with horticultural fleece or cloches.

**Dampen the soil** before thinning to make it easier to uproot seedlings.

4in (10cm)

4in (10cm)

**Sow or plant** in rows 4in (10cm) apart and thin or space plants the same distance apart.

# ③ Aftercare and harvest

Keep plants free of weeds and well-watered. Growth can turn lax and floppy once plants have matured, and you may need to provide support with twine tied and wrapped around canes positioned at the ends of rows.

Plants are ready to harvest in 6–8 weeks, depending on the soil and growing conditions; growth is slower in cooler conditions and when temperatures are too high. Cut leaves while they are still firm, leaving some growth above the soil to allow for multiple harvests. If you do this, the plant can be cut several times, and leaves will regrow. If you'd like to use the petal flowers as a garnish or in teas, leave a few plants and the ends of rows to grow on and produce flowers.

**Watering regularly** will promote tender growth and prevent plants running to flower at the expense of foliage.

## Cook's tips

### Keep fresh
Harvest in the morning when the weather is cool, put straight into a plastic bag, and store in the refrigerator.

### How to eat
The taste of garland daisies is particularly suited to Asian cuisine, but it also goes well with the robust flavors of Indian and Mediterranean dishes.

- Chop and add to stir-fries.
- Steam, blanch, or lightly boil and add to stews at the last minute; overcooking turns the leaves bitter.
- Use young, mild leaves raw in a Korean-style salad with soybean paste and toasted sesame seeds.
- Scatter over a Taiwanese oyster omelet and allow the leaves to just wilt.
- Fry with garlic and add lemon and pine nuts for a side dish.

### How to preserve
There are no worthwhile means of preserving the leaves, but the flowers can be dried and used in herbal teas.

## Quick guide

**Sow** under cover in late spring or outdoors in summer

**Minimum** 41°F (5°C) but grows best at 68°F (20°C) or above

**Grow** in light, well-drained soil in a sunny, sheltered position

**Water** only in dry weather

**Plants grow** up to 4ft (1.2m) in height and 19in (50cm) in spread

**Harvest** leaves regularly during summer and fall

# Callaloo

*Amaranthus leafy cultivars*

{ Level 2 moderate }

Callaloo is an incredibly colorful leaf crop, closely related to the summer bedding plant love-lies-bleeding. Mature and baby leaves are packed full of vitamins and calcium and cooked like spinach, although they have their own distinctive earthy flavor.

## What is it?

Callaloo is the name given both to amaranthus plants grown for their leaves and the Caribbean side dish cooked with them, but the leaves are also widely eaten in Asia, South America, and Africa. Amaranthus can also be grown to produce grain (see pp.136–39), and to avoid coarse leaves choose a cultivar selected for leaf quality, such as *Amaranthus* 'Red Army' or a cultivar of *A. tricolor*. Tender, heat-loving plants, they are grown as annuals in cooler climates and have an upright habit.

**Callaloo flowers** are smaller and more upright than the tassels of amaranthus grown for grains.

### When to grow and harvest

Given heat, callaloo is a fast-growing crop. Regular picking is essential to keep tender new leaves coming.

| | early winter | late winter | early spring | late spring | early summer | late summer | early fall | late fall |
|---|---|---|---|---|---|---|---|---|
| sow indoors | | | | • | • | | | |
| sow outdoors | | | | | • | • | | |
| plant out | | | | | • | • | | |
| harvest | | | | | | • | • | • |

## How do I grow it?

Callaloo grows best in temperatures above 68°F (20°C) and will not tolerate frost, so in temperate climates only a sheltered outdoor site will do. Delay sowing outdoors until summer, or start off indoors in late spring. Pot-raised plants are less vigorous, but can be planted out closer together to compensate.

## 1 Sow indoors

Sow early under cover to give these heat-lovers a head start. The tiny seeds are best mixed with sand to ease sowing. Sow ¼in (5mm) deep into large modules of well-drained, moist seed-starting mix. Place in a propagator at 68°F (20°C) and cover to encourage germination in the dark; seedlings should emerge in 14 days. Harden off (see p.62) and transplant outdoors when large enough to handle and the temperature is above 61°F (16°C).

## Cook's tips

### Keep fresh
To store, cut whole stems of leaves, wrap loosely in a plastic bag, and place in the refrigerator for up to 2 days.

### How to eat
Baby leaves are delicious raw in salads. Larger leaves are best cooked.

- Stew Caribbean-style with tomatoes, onions, and garlic.
- Fry with garlic, chilies, or cumin and include in Asian curries, dhals, and bhajees.
- Slice leaves to add wonderful color and flavor to soups, stews, and stir-fries.

### How to preserve
Lightly steam leaves, cool immediately, and freeze.

## ② Sow outdoors

Only sow outdoors when there is no longer a chance of frost. Warm the soil before sowing by covering with horticultural fleece for 2 weeks. Make drills 4in (10cm) apart for baby leaf crops or 12in (30cm) apart to grow more mature plants. Sow a seed and sand mixture at a depth of ¼in (5mm), then cover carefully with soil as well as fleece, if the weather is cool, to keep the soil temperature as high as possible. Germination may take upward of 3 weeks.

## ③ Thin out and harvest

Thin outdoor seedlings to 5–7in (13–18cm) apart, giving the larger cultivars more space to spread. Pot-grown plants will not be as vigorous, so give them 4in (10cm) space in rows 10in (25cm) apart. Once watered in well and established, plants need little attention. Cut baby leaves when plants reach 4in (10cm) high, and more mature leaves as required. Remove the top rosette to encourage sideshoots, and remove flowering shoots to maintain leaf growth.

{ Level 1 easy }

# Walking-stick kale

*Brassica oleracea var. longata*

This crazy vegetable with a head for heights is a variety of kale native to the Channel Islands, where it has traditionally been grown to make walking sticks, as well as for food. The towering stems can reach up to 10ft (3m) in one season, and the prolific topknot of leaves provides an endless supply of superfood greens.

## What is it?

Walking-stick kale is a biennial that grows stems and leaves in its first year, before flowering the next. Part of the brassica family of cabbage-type plants, it faces stiff competition in the quirkiness department from cousins grown variously for mutant side buds (sprouts), monstrous flower heads (cauliflower), and Martian-like swollen stems (kohlrabi). In an 1836 volume of *The Farmers' Magazine,* it was said that "these stupendous cabbages" are so nutritious, they "will speedily produce the most surprising improvement in the growth … of cattle." And what is good for the cow is surely good for the gardener.

*To make walking sticks, hang the stems for 1 year in a cool, well-ventilated place to dry out and harden, before sanding and varnishing.*

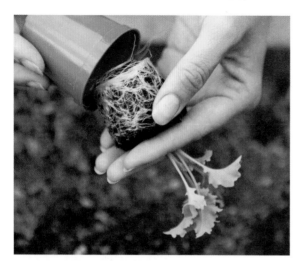

**Walking-stick kale** is a very hardy plant and seedlings raised under cover do not need to be hardened off before they are transplanted outdoors.

## How do I grow it?

Sow seeds under cover in early spring or outdoors in a seedbed for later transplanting. You will need to prep the soil before planting your seedlings: remove all weeds and make sure the soil is slightly alkaline by digging in lime if the pH is below 6.5. Growth is improved by adding well-rotted growing medium that is allowed to settle before planting, or where the soil has been improved for the previous crop, as the ground must be firm but not compacted. Net against cabbage white butterflies and pigeons, and support plants with stakes as they grow.

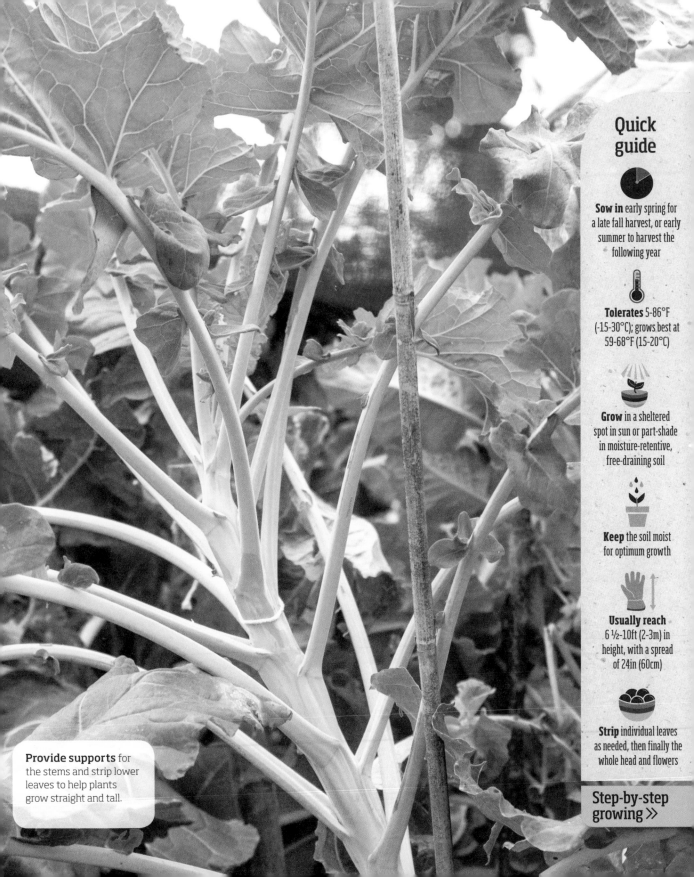

**Provide supports** for the stems and strip lower leaves to help plants grow straight and tall.

## Quick guide

**Sow in** early spring for a late fall harvest, or early summer to harvest the following year

**Tolerates** 5-86°F (-15-30°C); grows best at 59-68°F (15-20°C)

**Grow** in a sheltered spot in sun or part-shade in moisture-retentive, free-draining soil

**Keep** the soil moist for optimum growth

**Usually reach** 6 ½-10ft (2-3m) in height, with a spread of 24in (60cm)

**Strip** individual leaves as needed, then finally the whole head and flowers

**Step-by-step growing »**

# Step-by-step growing

Since walking-stick kale can grow to 10ft (3m) tall, plants need a spacious, open site and firm soil. Keep well watered at all times and net against pests for as long as possible.

### When to grow and harvest
Sow in spring for transplanting, and harvest a few leaves from each plant as it grows.

| | early winter | late winter | early spring | late spring | early summer | late summer | early fall | late fall |
|---|---|---|---|---|---|---|---|---|
| sow indoors | | | ● | ● | ● | | | |
| transplant | | | | ● | ● | | | |
| sow outdoors | | | | ● | ● | | | |
| harvest | | | | | | | ● | ● | ● |

## 1 Sow indoors

To guard against clubroot, a common disease of brassicas, it is best to raise your own plants rather than buy in from unreliable sources. Sow seeds 1in (2.5cm) deep in modules filled with seed-starting mix. Germination takes about 10 days. Before they start to outgrow the modules, pot up to individual pots filled with all-purpose mix; don't allow seedlings to become pot-bound. Kale is extremely hardy, and there is no need to acclimatize seedlings before planting out.

**Take care** when handling the seedlings, as the roots are easily damaged.

## 2 Plant out

Seedlings should be ready to plant out 6 weeks after sowing. Water well and transplant to leave 32in (80cm) between plants and rows. Ensure the lowest leaf is touching the soil so the base of the stem is buried. Firm in the soil and water copiously to leave a puddle at the base of each plant. Alternatively, sow outdoors 3in (7.5cm) apart in a finely raked seedbed and thin to the same spacings. Fit cabbage collars around the base of stems to protect from cabbage root fly; these are discs 5in (13cm) in diameter with a slit cut to the center and can be made of carpet underlay or similar.

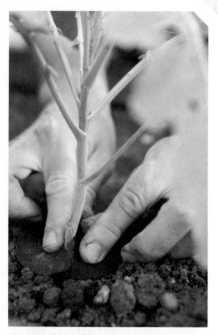

**Ensure the collar** is flat on the ground to prevent the adult cabbage root fly laying its eggs at the base of the stem.

32in (80cm)

32in (80cm)

**Leave plenty** of space between plants so the huge leaves aren't restricted.

# 3 Protection and aftercare

It is important to protect plants from the attentions of pigeons, which can strip young plants entirely, and of the caterpillars of cabbage butterflies and moths, which chomp many unsightly holes in leaves. Cover plants with horticultural fleece, or build a frame with stakes for fine mesh netting. Allow a gap between the net and leaves so the adult insects cannot reach the leaves to lay their eggs. Keep plants weed free and well watered. Feed a general fertilizer if growth looks sluggish, but do not overfeed, as this makes the plants soft and the leaves prone to tearing. Stake and tie in plants as they grow.

**Make sure the mesh** of the net is fine enough to protect against small insects, such as cabbage white butterflies.

# 4 Harvest and end of season

Harvest leaves as needed, stripping the lower leaves first and working up the stem to the canopy at the top. At the end of the growing season, you have a choice: dig up and compost the plants; retain the stems and dry them out to fashion, Jersey-style, into walking sticks (they also make good plant supports); or leave these biennials to grow a second year, when they will produce flowers, which are edible and a source of nectar for bees.

## Cook's tips

**Keep fresh**
Store the leaves in a sealed plastic bag in the refrigerator.

**How to eat**
Cook in the same way as ordinary kale and cabbage: chop and steam, boil, stir-fry, or braise. The flowers are also edible.

- Blend with fruit, coconut water, and spices for an energy-boosting smoothie.
- Roll whole leaves around a filling of rice and mince and bake in a tomato sauce.
- Pot-roast with game birds.
- Combine steamed leaves with fried pancetta, navy beans, and cream, sprinkle with breadcrumbs and cheese, and bake for a hearty gratin.
- Stir shredded leaves into soups, stews, or curries for the last five minutes of cooking.
- Pick the flowers and scatter in salads.

**How to preserve**
Rinse leaves and pat dry with paper towel, then freeze in bags for up to two months. Shredded leaves can also be salted and fermented for sauerkraut.

## Quick guide

**Sow** under cover in early spring or outdoors once soil has warmed

**Ideal range** 50-86°F (10-30°C) or more; good crop for hot climates

**Grow** in full sun or part-shade in any well-drained soil

**Keep plants** well watered

**Plants grow** up to 3ft (1m) high and spread to 18in (45cm)

**Harvest** leaves when young and pick flower heads just before the flowers open

**Level 1** easy

# Huauzontle

*Chenopodium nuttalliae*

This productive, unfussy crop tastes like broccoli and is far easier to grow. No wonder it is such a popular vegetable in Mexico, where locals snack on cheesy fritters made from the unopened flowers. The name is pronounced "wow-zon-telay," but you could just call it Aztec broccoli.

## What is it?

This member of the Goosefoot family of plants, which includes red orach, amaranth, and beets, can grow into large bushes 3ft (1m) or more tall and wide. It is believed to share the same parentage as quinoa, another crop in the *Chenopodium* genus, but was used for its leaves and shoots rather than seeds, and was developed in the hot, dry regions of Mexico to grow among the corn stems. As they mature, plants undergo an intriguing color change from green to yellow and pink.

### When to grow and harvest

Sow seeds early and plants will be mature enough for harvesting at the beginning of summer.

| | early winter | late winter | early spring | late spring | early summer | late summer | early fall | late fall |
|---|---|---|---|---|---|---|---|---|
| sow indoors | | | • | • | • | | | |
| sow outdoors | | | | | • | • | • | • |
| plant out | | | | | • | • | | |
| harvest | | | | | | • | • | • |

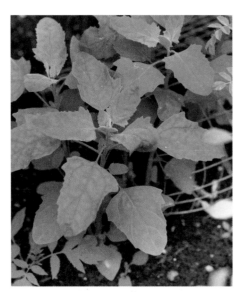

**Huauzontle** grows quickly, and its unopened flower heads and leaves can be harvested in as little as 7 weeks after sowing.

## How do I grow it?

Huauzontle is easily grown from seed and will flourish in hot weather, making it an ideal crop for warmer climates. Plants are productive even in poorer soils, but more prolific if you enrich the planting site by digging in plenty of organic matter. Be warned: seedlings are almost identical to the edible weed lamb's quarters, so be careful not to pull them out by mistake!

###  1 Sow seeds

Sow indoors from early spring in modules. Given warm conditions, seeds should germinate in just 3 or 4 days. Once all risk of frost has passed, harden off seedlings (see p.62) and plant outdoors with 12in (30cm) distance between plants and rows. Handle carefully and try to avoid root disturbance. You can also sow directly outside onto a finely raked seedbed; sow more than you need and thin to 12in (30cm) between plants.

## Cook's tips

### Keep fresh

Flower heads, leaves, and shoots will store for a couple of days in a plastic bag in the refrigerator.

### How to eat

Steam or blanch in boiling water; all parts hold their texture well.

- Make traditional Mexican fritters: mix grated cheese and eggs with cooked huauzontle, form into patties, and fry until golden. Serve with a tomato or chili sauce.
- Add fresh to stir-fries, curries, and stews.

### How to preserve

All parts can be blanched, quickly cooled, and frozen.

## ② Aftercare

Give plants a feed of liquid seaweed and keep them well watered until established. Protect from pigeons with horticultural fleece or netting when the plants are small. Slugs and snails may also be a problem: try using organic controls such as garlic sprays, beer traps, and nematodes, and encourage natural predators (ground beetles, toads, and so on). Plants may need supporting on windy sites with stakes or canes.

## ③ Harvest

Harvest the tiny flower heads before they open, and gather leaves from the top 4in (10cm) of each flowering stem, picking a few leaves from each plant to avoid a check in growth. Plants quickly produce more side stems for further harvests. Pick the leaves before they start to turn a deep red color, after which they take on a bitter taste. Young shoots can also be eaten.

# Salsola

**Level 2** *moderate*

*Salsola soda, S. komarovii*

Bring the flavors of the foraged seashore to your garden with one of the best-kept culinary secrets of Italy and Japan. The succulent leaves of salsola have a crisp bite and salty tang that make it an excellent alternative to samphire and seaweed.

## What is it?

Plants in the genus *Salsola* are found growing throughout Asia, North Africa, and the Mediterranean. In Italy, *Salsola soda*, commonly called "agretti," is a regional delicacy sold fresh in the markets of Umbria and Lazio, while in Japan, the lower-growing *S. komarovii* or "okahijiki" is immensely popular. Also known as "land seaweed" or "saltwort," these are short-leaved, salt-tolerant plants that grow in grassy clumps, like chives. Plants are found on coastal salt marshes in the wild, but you don't need to live by the sea to cultivate it at home.

### When to grow and harvest

Sow early and pick the young shoots or leave to mature before harvesting from late spring.

| | early winter | late winter | early spring | late spring | early summer | late summer | early fall | late fall |
|---|---|---|---|---|---|---|---|---|
| sow indoors | | | ● | ● | ● | | | |
| sow outdoors | | | | ● | ● | ● | ● | |
| plant out | | | | ● | ● | | | |
| harvest | | | | ● | ● | ● | ● | ● |

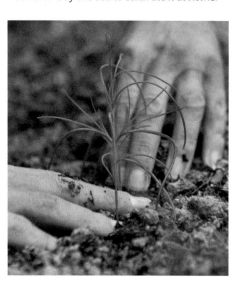

**After sowing indoors,** you can transplant seedlings outdoors, but only when any risk of frost has passed.

## How do I grow it?

Salsola tolerates poor soil, but prefers alkaline conditions and needs warmth to germinate and sunlight to flourish. Plants are best raised from seed, but the germination rate is notoriously low. Buy fresh seed, sow plenty, and be ready to sow as soon as the seed arrives.

###  1 Sow indoors

Although not a heat-loving plant, seeds need warm temperatures to germinate and are best started off under cover in a heated propagator set to 73–79°F (23–26°C). Sow seeds ¼in (5mm) deep in pots or modules filled with seed-starting mix. Seeds tend to germinate in 7 to 10 days, but occasionally take a little longer. Repot seedlings in larger pots as needed.

### Keep fresh
Store in plastic bags in the refrigerator for up to 1 week.

### How to eat
Eat young leaves raw in salads. Larger leaves are steamed, added to stir-fries, boiled, or blanched.

- Braise in olive oil and garlic and serve as a side dish.
- Chop and use to flavor a sauce for fish or seafood.
- Make a salad with tomatoes, lemon, garlic, and herbs.
- Try Japanese-style with sushi rice, crab, and egg.

### How to preserve
Pickle by packing leaves into an airtight storage jar and covering with brine.

## 2 Plant out or grow outdoors

Transplant indoor-raised seedlings to their growing area outdoors, spacing them 6in (15cm) apart. Further crops can be sown directly outdoors if the soil is warm enough for germination. Rake a level seedbed and sow ¼in (5mm) deep in rows 4in (10cm) apart, or broadcast the seed. When the seedlings have developed a few sets of leaves, thin them to 6in (15cm) apart; you can eat the thinnings!

## 3 Aftercare and harvest

Remove any weeds and keep plants well watered for the plumpest leaves; watering with slightly salted water is not essential, but it does make a difference to the taste. Feed a general fertilizer to boost growth only if needed. Leaves can be harvested as a cut-and-come-again crop by shearing off the tops to encourage plenty of young, tender regrowth. Stop harvesting when plants begin to flower.

# ROOTS, BULBS, AND SHOOTS

# Yacón

**Level 2** moderate

*Smallanthus sonchifolius*

If you like the texture of water chestnuts and the taste of watermelon and pear, then try growing yacón. Sweet, crisp, crunchy, and juicy, the delicious tubers well deserve their alternative name of Peruvian ground apple, and can be eaten raw as a snack, roasted, or added to stir-fries.

## Quick guide

**Start off under cover** in spring for planting out after the last frosts

**Minimum** 32°F (0°C) to maximum 86°F (30°C)

**Will crop** in poor soil but prefers deep, rich soil; needs a sunny, sheltered spot

**Drought-tolerant,** but water well in dry spells to ensure large tubers

**Grows** up to 8ft (2.5m) high and spreads up to 3ft 3in (1m)

**Lift tubers** after the first frosts

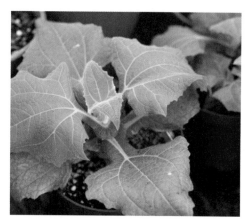

**Usually grown as a perennial** for its tubers, yacón can also be grown as an annual plant and harvested for its edible young main stems.

## What is it?

Yacón has been cultivated as a crop in South America for 2,000 years and can be found growing in the Andes up to elevations of 9,843ft (3,000m). The root system of each plant is made up of large, plump tubers, which are dug up for eating, and smaller knobby roots, which can be stored over winter and replanted the following spring. The sweetness in the tubers comes from a type of sugar called inulin, which is not easily broken down by the body. This means you can enjoy a sweet hit without the calories, but may end up feeling a little gassy.

## How do I grow it?

Yacón will thrive in most soils where there is reasonable rainfall and a good amount of sunlight, but they do need plenty of space to spread out, making them unsuitable for growing in pots. Although a long growing season is required for a decent harvest, unlike many South American root crops, the plants do not need short days before forming tubers, and so can be grown more easily in northerly latitudes. You need to position them in a sunny area, however, as the heat-to-light ratio must be correct: too much heat and too little light means "leggy" plants. Yacón is a distant relative of the sunflower and, with its huge fuzzy leaves and attractive yellow flowers, looks good in the flower border or the vegetable patch.

*In Spanish colonial times, yacón tubers became a staple food for sailors, who found they stored extremely well over the long transatlantic crossings.*

**The flesh** of the tubers ranges in color from white to pale yellow and orange to purple.

Step-by-step growing »

# Step-by-step growing

Yacón should be grown in moist, well-drained soil rich in organic matter. In temperate zones this plant bursts into growth after the summer solstice, and from then on has an increased requirement for water.

### When to grow and harvest
Start tubers into growth in early spring and harvest when the foliage is blackened after the first frosts.

| | early winter | late winter | early spring | late spring | early summer | late summer | early fall | late fall |
|---|---|---|---|---|---|---|---|---|
| plant indoors | | | ● | ● | | | | |
| plant out | | | | ● | ● | | | |
| harvest | | | | | | | ● | ● |

## ① Plant indoors

Start plants off under cover in early spring. Fill 6in (15cm) pots with rich potting mix and plant a tuber in each pot just below the surface. Place in a greenhouse at around 68°F (20°C), or on a warm windowsill. A combination of too much heat and too little light causes the stems to become leggy; such plants will never thrive, so balance the ratio of light to heat by placing the plants in a bright area.

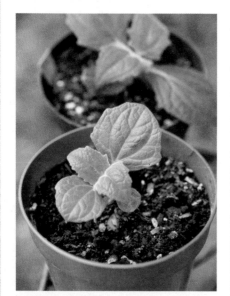

**The first shoots** may be yellow, white, or even colorless, but this is quite normal and tubers will soon put on leafy growth.

## ② Plant out

Transplant the tubers into larger pots if necessary. Acclimate the young plants to the colder temperatures outside by placing them in a cloche or cold frame and gradually increasing ventilation, first during the day and then also at night.

When the soil is warm and there is no further risk of frost, plant them in their final positions, leaving about 3ft (90cm) between plants and the same distance between rows. Yacón is a hungry crop and will benefit from having well-rotted manure or other organic matter dug into the soil before planting.

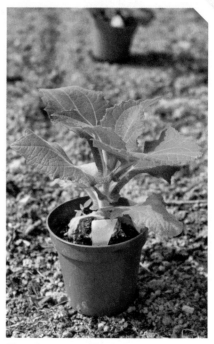

**Give the young plants** a good soak both before and after planting.

3ft (90cm)

3ft (90cm)

**Plants ultimately** put on lots of tall, leafy growth and need to be spaced well apart.

## 3 Aftercare

Protect young plants from late frosts and cold snaps with cloches or horticultural fleece. Once established, these resilient plants aren't much bothered by pests or diseases, but you may need to pick off slugs and snails from lower leaves.

Yacón grows slowly at first, and it's worth planting a quick crop of radishes, spinach, or lettuce in the space around them, not least to help suppress weeds. Keep plants thoroughly watered once they go into overdrive in midsummer. Yacón stems can reach a height of over 6½ft (2m), and on windy sites plants may need to be given some support.

**Provide support** by tying plants individually to canes or stakes, or by running string around stakes positioned at the perimeter of the planting area.

## 4 Harvest and propagation

Once the first frosts have blackened the foliage, lift the plants carefully to avoid damaging the tubers. You will find two sets of tubers: the large storage tubers, which are for eating, and above them in the crown of the plant are the smaller rooting tubers, from which you can propagate next year's crop. After removing the large tubers, cut back the stems to about 3in (7.5cm), transfer each crown to a box or large pot of moistened potting mix, and store over winter in a cool but frost-free place under cover. New shoots will start to appear next spring. When they do, cut out each tuber with its shoot, ready for the next crop.

**Propagate** next year's crop from the small tubers at the top.

# Quick guide

**Plant bulbs** in early fall in their final flowering positions

**Minimum** 30°F (-1°C) to maximum 77°F (25°C)

**Grow** in clay or moist, free-draining soil in sun or part-shade; prefers a dry rest

**Keep moist** during the growing season in spring, but can dry out in summer

**Plants grow** up to 4ft (1.25m) in height and 32in (80cm) in spread

**Dig up bulbs** when the stems die down in summer, or all year round after flowering

**{ Level 1 easy }**

# Camas

*Camassia quamash*

Camas bulbs were once an important wild harvest for Native Americans in North America, who would bake them *en masse* in fire pits. Be warned: they are the ultimate slow-food vegetable, taking anything from 12-48 hours to cook—but the sublime taste is worth the effort.

## What is it?

Native across much of western Canada and the northwestern US, camas is a long-lived perennial bulb, coming back year after year to produce spectacular, dense spikes of vivid blue, starry flowers in late spring. Establish a large clump in the garden; you can then lift some to eat when they die down and replant the others. Bake overnight or steam in a slow cooker until the pale bulbs have turned a deep chestnut brown. After cooking, they taste somewhere between baked figs, roasted chestnuts, and caramelized onions.

### When to grow and harvest

Camas are perennial; once planted, they can be harvested annually, and you can enjoy the pretty blue spring flowers, too.

| | early winter | late winter | early spring | late spring | early summer | late summer | early fall | late fall |
|---|---|---|---|---|---|---|---|---|
| plant bulbs | | | | | | | • | • |
| harvest | | | | | • | | | |

**Harvest bulbs** that are 1-2in (2.5-5cm) in diameter in early summer, after the flowers have died back.

## How do I grow it?

In its native habitat, camas is found in wet prairies and meadows that often dry out by late spring. Aim to replicate that environment in the garden with humus-rich soil that retains moisture but is not waterlogged in winter. If you experience a dry spring, water the plants until the foliage dies down.

### ① Prepare the soil

If necessary, improve the soil before planting to make it more moisture-retentive and free-draining. Incorporate well-rotted organic matter, such as homemade growing medium or soil conditioner from the garden center, forking it into the soil surface or taking the opportunity to dig over the ground. If the soil is sandy, mulching annually with a thick layer of well-rotted growing medium is essential, too.

## 2 Plant bulbs

Buy plump, healthy, undamaged bulbs for fall planting. Scatter bulbs randomly for a natural effect, planting them where they fall. Plant 3–8in (8–20cm) deep, twice the depth of the bulb and the same distance apart. Camas can also be grown in large, deep pots of moisture-retentive potting mix, with a layer of drainage material at the base. Protect the pots from frost in a garden shed or garage, at the base of a sheltered wall, or under a hedge–but don't forget about them!

## 3 Aftercare

Water plants in the ground in spring if dry. For pot-grown camas, start watering in spring to encourage growth and keep pots well watered, but allow them to dry out once the leaves have died back, mimicking what happens in nature. Feed camas in pots high-potassium fertilizer in spring and after flowering. Protect bulbs over winter with a thick layer of mulch on the soil surface, and move pot-grown plants to a cool but sheltered site under cover.

**Tubers come** in a range of shapes and sizes, from knobby to rounded to long and slender.

**Level 2**
*moderate*

# Dahlia yam
*Dahlia cultivars*

What, eat a dahlia? Yes, you can! The petals of the flowers can be added to salads as a colorful garnish, and the sweet, starchy, nutty-tasting tubers can be peeled and enjoyed raw or cooked. Just be sure to save a few large tubers for planting again next spring.

## What is it?

Dahlias are perennial plants that grow from tubers to produce a vibrant summer display of large, colorful flowers, before dying back in fall, ready to sprout again in the spring. Native to Mexico and Central America, dahlias were first grown by the Aztecs for their sweet-potato-like tubers, and Spanish conquistadors brought them back to Europe in the 16th century as an edible root crop. The Victorians decided dahlias were better suited to the flower border than the vegetable patch, and that's where they stayed—until now!

> *The Aztecs of ancient Mexico used the dried hollow stems of "tree dahlias" (Dahlia imperialis) as pipes for plumbing and irrigation.*

*Dahlia* 'Black Jack' bears dark crimson semi-cactus blooms and produces tubers with red skins and smooth flesh.

## How do I grow it?

First you need to pick the right variety, as there are hundreds available and some are tastier than others. Cactus-flowered varieties are generally a good bet, producing the mightiest tubers, as well as the largest flowers; "DeliDahlia" cultivars have been developed especially for eating. If growing in an ornamental border, be aware that a fair proportion of blooms must be removed if you want to enjoy a sizable harvest of tubers. In milder areas, tubers can be left in the ground to overwinter, but in regions where the ground becomes frozen in winter, they will need to be lifted and stored under cover.

## Quick guide

**Plant out** tubers after the last frosts; bring stored plants into growth in late winter

**Minimum** 23°F (-5°C) to maximum 77°F (25°C)

**Grow in** a sunny spot in organic-rich, free-draining soil

**Tubers** have a high water content and need lots of watering

**Plants** can reach 3ft (1m) high and spread 16in (40cm)

**Harvest** tubers in fall when the foliage is blackened by the first frost

**Step-by-step growing »**

# Step-by-step growing

Dahlias are sold in most garden centers, so they should be easy to find. They need rich soil, a sheltered site, and the support of a stake. Provide plenty of water throughout the growing season, but do not overfeed.

**When to grow and harvest**
Dahlias need a long growing season: plant in late spring and harvest in fall.

| | early winter | late winter | early spring | late spring | early summer | late summer | early fall | late fall |
|---|---|---|---|---|---|---|---|---|
| plant out | | | | ● | ● | | | |
| harvest | | | | | | | ● | ● |

## 1 Prepare your plants

When the dahlia crowns sprout shoots ¾–1¼in (2–3cm) high in spring, divide them into smaller clusters of tubers or individual sections, ensuring each section has roots and shoots. You can then either plant outside immediately, if your climate is warm enough (see step 2), or pot in separate containers filled with potting mix and grow on under cover until risk of frost has passed.

Alternatively, take cuttings of the new shoots of sprouted tubers when they are 2–3in (5–7.5cm) long, retaining a small piece of tuber. Trim the leaves from the base of each cutting, dip in rooting powder, and plant in a free-draining potting mix. Keep at 70°F (21°C) until they root, then repot individually into 3½in (9cm) pots filled with potting mix. Plants grown from cuttings are usually stronger and healthier.

## 2 Plant out

A few weeks before planting, incorporate plenty of well-rotted organic matter into the soil and allow to settle. At the same time, if you have grown plants under cover, harden them off to outdoor conditions (see p.62). To plant, push a stake or cane into the ground to provide a support for each dahlia as it grows. Leave a space of 3–4ft (90–120cm) between plants. Dig a hole at the base of each support 4–6in (10–15cm) deep and slightly larger than the section or cluster of tubers. Backfill with soil and firm in, leaving a slight saucer-shaped depression to hold water.

**Position the tubers** or young plants so they are right up against the support.

3–4ft (90–120cm)

3–4ft (90–120cm)

**Space plants** at 3–4ft (90–120cm) intervals in rows the same distance apart.

# 3 Aftercare

Keep plants well watered: the ground should be constantly moist. Dahlias also need protection from slugs and snails and there are a variety of environmentally friendly ways: encourage predators like ground beetles, frogs, toads, and thrushes; use nematodes; lay a sheet of burlap or plastic on the ground, or an upturned, hollowed-out grapefruit, then collect and dispose of them by hand; or douse plants with garlic spray.

Start feeding with high-potash fertilizer when you notice that the flower buds are beginning to develop. Leave some buds to bloom, but prune out the majority, as the plants' energies are better spent increasing the size of the tubers.

**Dahlia flowers are too pretty** to sacrifice entirely, but most should be nipped in the bud.

# 4 Lift and store

Once the first frosts have blackened the foliage, cut stems back to within 2in (5cm) of the base and carefully lift the tubers. Move any clusters not being used immediately to a dry, cool, frost-free location. To discourage rot, turn the clusters upside down for a few weeks so water drains from the hollow stems. Retain one cluster of each variety from which to propagate next season's crop.

**Store an entire cluster** of tubers from each variety. These can then be divided and planted outside, or grown under cover, when shoots emerge the following spring.

## Cook's tips

### Keep fresh
Store the tubers as you would potatoes, in a cool, dark, dry place.

### How to eat
The tubers can be eaten either raw or cooked. The edible flowers are also tasty as a garnish or chopped up in salads.

- Peel, cube, steam till tender, then mash with lots of butter.
- Toss with oil, honey, and rosemary and roast with other root vegetables or on their own.
- Grate and combine with egg, flour, chopped onions, and herbs to form cakes, then pan-fry till golden.
- Cut into very thin slices, then fry or oven-bake to make sweet-tasting crisps.
- Make a winter-warming soup enriched with cream and spiced with cinnamon.

### How to preserve
Blemish-free tubers store for long periods in a cool, dark, airy place. Do not store where dry air encourages drying out. Check regularly and eat any showing the first signs of shriveling.

**There is no need to peel** mashua tubers before cooking: the skin is nutty, nutritious, and not at all tough.

# Mashua

*Tropaeolum tuberosum*

**Level 1 easy**

With long twining stems, attractive gray-green leaves, and showy flowers, mashua will look wonderful in the vegetable patch climbing over a trellis. Eaten raw, the tubers have a peppery, aniseed flavor, which becomes milder when cooked. The leaves and flowers are also edible and make a great addition to salads.

## What is it?

A close relative of the garden nasturtium *Tropaeolum majus*, mashua is a bushy, scrambling plant native to the Andes Mountains in South America, where they have long been valued as a crop for their ease of cultivation, resistance to disease, and ability to be left in the ground and harvested as needed. The tubers are the size of small potatoes and vary in color from cream to purple-striped. Outside of South America, mashua is more commonly grown as a garden ornamental, with cultivar 'Ken Aslet' a popular choice.

Mashua was used in traditional medicine to suppress the libido, and Inca emperors fed it to their armies "that they should forget their wives."

**Cultivar 'Ken Aslet'** bears attractive orange flowers with long red spurs.

## How do I grow it?

Mashua flourishes in warm rather than scorching hot summers and needs a long growing season, since the tubers of most varieties only start to form when the period of daylight is 12 hours or less. The cultivar 'Ken Aslet', however, will form tubers regardless of the length of daylight. Mashua is suitable for growing up netting, wire fencing, or an upright column, but they don't climb well on a tripod of canes unless you wrap string around it. Alternatively, allow them to scramble over the ground. They can also be grown in large pots or barrels of moisture-retentive potting mix.

## Quick guide

**Plant out** tubers once the danger of frost has passed

**Minimum** 39°F (4°C) to maximum 68°F (20°C)

**Grow** in moist, rich, well-drained soil in a sheltered sunny or partially shady spot

**Water well** during the growing season or they will go dormant

**Plants climb** up to 8–12ft (2.5–4m) and spread up to 3ft (1m)

**Cut back** foliage after the first frost and lift the tubers

**Step-by-step growing »**

# Step-by-step growing

Start tubers into growth under cover in cooler climates. Plant outdoors in rich soil and keep it constantly moist. Mashua will tolerate a part-shaded position as it doesn't like to get too hot in summer.

## When to grow and harvest

Mashua is a long-season crop; plant in spring and harvest when the stems are cut back by fall frosts.

| | early winter | late winter | early spring | late spring | early summer | late summer | early fall | late fall |
|---|---|---|---|---|---|---|---|---|
| plant indoors | | | ● | ● | | | | |
| plant out | | | | ● | ● | | | |
| harvest | | | | | | | ● | ● |

## 1 Plant indoors

Start mashua off in early spring by planting tubers 1¼in (3cm) deep in individual pots filled with moist potting mix. Place somewhere warm and bright and keep the mix moistened. Meanwhile, clear weeds and stones from the planting ground outdoors and, 2 or 3 weeks before planting, dig in plenty of well-rotted organic matter to improve nutrition and drainage. Allow to settle.

**Mice love to eat** the tubers, and you will need to provide protection, such as a glass or plastic barrier, if growing in a greenhouse.

## 2 Plant out

Once the danger of frost has passed, plant young plants outside with 12in (30cm) space all round, and water well. You can also plant tubers directly outdoors at the same time, 1¼in (3cm) deep and 12in (30cm) apart. Plants can be slow to emerge, especially in colder areas, and it's worth covering with cloches or horticultural fleece to encourage growth. Also consider raising a crop of fast-growing vegetables like spinach, lettuce, or radish in the space between plants, harvesting before the mashua sprouts.

**A thick mulch** of well-rotted organic matter will help boost growth, retain moisture, and cool the roots.

12in (30cm)

12in (30cm)

**Leave 12in (30cm)** between young plants and tubers, and the same distance between rows.

## ③ Aftercare

Protect young plants from slugs and snails by one or more environmentally friendly methods, such as dousing with garlic spray, using nematodes, and laying organic traps. Keep the area weed free until plants are established, when the foliage of these vigorous scrambling plants will act as a weed suppressant. Provide plants with climbing support, such as netting, rings of fencing wire, hazel sticks, or canes. Water constantly to plump up the tubers; plants go dormant if the soil dries out for long periods.

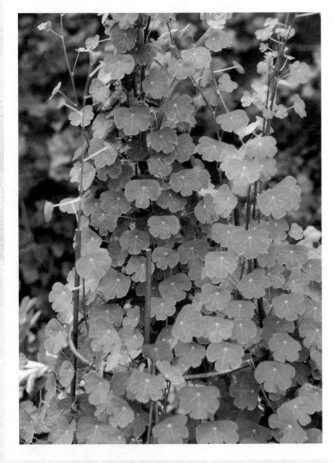

**Mashua will** happily scramble over free-standing circular supports, or can be trained up canes and sticks.

## ④ Harvest

Lift tubers in fall after the first frosts. Clean the soil from the tubers and make sure they are dry before storing in a cool, dry, frost-free place. Retain some medium-sized tubers for planting the following year, but exclude those of plants affected by mosaic virus, which manifests as a patterned mottling on leaves.

**Lift plants** carefully and eat any damaged tubers as soon as possible.

### Cook's tips

**Keep fresh**

Store somewhere cool and dark, but not in the fridge.

**How to eat**

Eaten raw and straight out of the ground or storage, the tubers are pleasantly spicy, but if cooked or left in a sunny spot for a week or so, they develop a much sweeter taste. Leaves and flowers can also be eaten.

- Slice raw tubers and eat them like radishes in salads.
- Add leaves and flowers to salads for the same spicy kick as watercress and arugula.
- Cook tubers as you would potatoes: boiled, mashed, sautéed, or roasted.
- Fry parboiled cubes in butter with bacon and shallots, stir in a handful of the leaves, and pour over beaten egg for an Andean frittata.

**How to preserve**

Blemish-free tubers store for long periods in a cool, dark, airy place. Check regularly and eat any with signs of shriveling. Do not store where dry air causes drying out, or where light and warmth may start the tubers into growth.

## Quick guide

**Plant** tubers from late fall until early spring, while dormant

**Minimum** 5°F (-15°C) to 86°F (30°C) or higher

**Grow** in moisture-retentive, light, free-draining soil in full sun

**Water** to prevent soil drying out

**Plants grow** up to 20in (50cm) in height and 18in (45cm) in spread

**Harvest** as required from late fall until late winter

{ **Level 1** easy }

# Chinese artichoke

*Stachys affinis*

Easy to grow and similar in flavor to the Jerusalem artichoke but without the hugely tall growth and (ahem) associated digestive issues, the Chinese artichoke is well worth a try, especially in smaller gardens. And don't let the odd, segmented appearance of the plump, little grublike tubers put you off.

## What is it?

A perennial member of the mint family, the Chinese artichoke is native to wet ground in regions of China but is cultivated for its creamy-colored tubers all over eastern Asia. The tubers are also popular in French cooking, where they are called *crosnes*, and the plant is gradually becoming more widely known in the West. Attractive mounds of slightly furry, mintlike foliage make it a handsome addition to a vegetable patch or decorative border.

### When to grow and harvest

Plant tubers at any time while dormant. The new harvest will not be ready until late fall.

| | early winter | late winter | early spring | late spring | early summer | late summer | early fall | late fall |
|---|---|---|---|---|---|---|---|---|
| plant outdoors | • | • | • | | | | | • |
| earth up stems | | | | | • | | | |
| harvest | • | • | | | | | | • |

**The purple flowers** are a magnet for bees in summer, but are often pinched out to divert the plant's energy toward the tubers.

## How do I grow it?

Given good soil in full sun, the Chinese artichoke is trouble-free to grow. Tubers can be planted outdoors at any time while dormant, as long as the soil is not frozen. Plants start into growth early, when temperatures reach 41°F (5°C), and grow quickly in moisture-retentive soils to provide good ground cover.

###  1 Plant outdoors

Work plenty of well-rotted growing medium into the soil before planting. Plant dormant tubers from late fall until early spring. Place them with their points upward, about 3in (8cm) deep and 12in (30cm) apart, leaving 18in (45cm) between rows. Cover with soil and wait for shoots to emerge in spring. Alternatively, tubers can be started into growth under cover in pots filled with moist potting mix and planted out when their shoots are 4in (10cm) long.

## ② Aftercare

Protect the new shoots from slugs and snails and keep plants well-watered at all stages of growth. On light soils, apply a thick mulch of potting mix in early spring to help retain moisture. Earth up the stems in summer when they reach about 12in (30cm) tall to initiate the growth of as many tubers as possible. Pretty as they are, you should pinch back most of the flowers to concentrate the plant's energy into tuber formation, but try to leave a few for the bees!

## ③ Harvest

Chinese artichokes can be harvested at any time from late fall until they begin sprouting in early spring, but they taste sweeter once there has been a frost on the ground. Cut the plant's top growth back as it dies away in late fall and simply unearth tubers as required. In cold areas, mulch with the old stems to help keep the soil workable. Leaving a few tubers in the soil after harvest will produce new plants to supply the following year's crop.

{ Level 2 moderate }

# Oca
*Oxalis tuberosa*

This fascinating root crop is a delicious alternative to potatoes, producing good yields of colorful tubers that are about the size of new potatoes. Unlike potatoes, oca is not affected by blight, but it can struggle to produce well in cold climates because the plant is frost tender and the tubers don't develop until late fall.

## What is it?

Oca originated in the central Andean region of South America, where it has been widely cultivated for centuries and remains an important crop. The plant was also introduced to New Zealand in the 19th century, where it has become a popular staple and is known as New Zealand yam. Numerous cultivars are available, which produce tubers with different-colored skins, ranging from white to purple. All types can be eaten raw or cooked, and the crisp flesh has a slightly sharp sour-apple tang, which is more pronounced in some varieties than in others.

*The tubers' sharp taste comes from oxalates in their skin, chemical compounds that can be reduced by leaving them in sunlight before eating.*

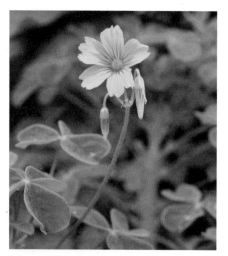

**Oca is an attractive crop** with bright yellow flowers and lush foliage consisting of large, clover-shaped leaves.

## How do I grow it?

Oca is a tender perennial which, like potatoes, is grown as an annual crop, although its preferred longer, frost-free growing season can be a challenge in cooler regions. Before planting the tubers, first encourage them to start sprouting by placing them in a light, cool, but frost-free place (the same process as sprouting potatoes). Once sprouted, either plant the tubers in rows directly outdoors when the risk of frost has passed, or give them a head start by planting in pots to begin growth indoors. Once in the ground, oca plants need little attention aside from earthing up to encourage tuber formation, which is initiated by the shortening lengths of the days in fall. Don't unearth the tubers until the foliage has been cut back by frost. If the frosts arrive too early, the plant may die and not grow any tubers, so listen to the weather forecast and cover with horticultural fleece if needed.

Oca tubers come in various colors, depending on cultivar, including pink, purple, yellow, and white.

## Quick guide

**Plant indoors** in early spring, or outdoors once the risk of frost has passed

**Minimum** 39°F (4°C) to ideally 68°F (20°C), but tolerates higher

**Grow** in well-drained soil in full sun

**Water** during dry spells, especially as tubers form in fall

**Plants grow** up to 20in (50cm) high and 12in (30cm) wide

**Harvest** in early winter when foliage has been frosted

Step-by-step growing »

# Step-by-step growing

Wider spacing allows these bushy plants to produce higher yields of tubers and to spread by rooting their stems into the soil. Don't worry, though; oca is not invasive like some other members of the *Oxalis* genus.

### When to grow and harvest

If you have a short growing season between spring and fall frosts, get a head start by planting tubers indoors.

| | early winter | late winter | early spring | late spring | early summer | late summer | early fall | late fall |
|---|---|---|---|---|---|---|---|---|
| plant indoors | | | ● | ● | | | | |
| plant out | | | | ● | ● | | | |
| earth up | | | | | | ● | ● | |
| harvest | ● | ● | | | | | | |

## 1 Plant indoors

Tubers start sprouting from mid- to late winter. When they do, space them out on a tray in sunlight to sprout and slow further growth. If left in the dark, they produce long, fragile shoots that break on planting. In cooler climates with a risk of spring frosts, plant each tuber about 3in (8cm) deep in moistened all-purpose potting mix in a 6in (15cm) pot. Grow in the greenhouse or on a sunny windowsill.

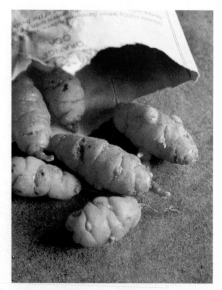

**Store tubers** in a cool, frost-free place and check for signs of growth.

## 2 Plant out

When all risk of frost has passed, if planting tubers directly outdoors, make drills about 3in (8cm) deep and 36in (90cm) apart. Then plant the tubers along the drills, spacing them 18in (45cm) apart. Gently rake soil back over the drills and then cover with a layer of fleece to help warm the soil.

If you have started plants off under cover, harden off the young plants to the colder temperatures outside by placing them in a cloche or cold frame and gradually increasing ventilation, first during the day and then also at night. Plant outside at the same spacings.

**A string guideline** and rod or stick with measurements marked on it are useful tools when planting in rows.

36in (90cm)

18in (45cm)

**Wide spacing** allows these bushy plants to produce higher yields of tubers.

## ③ Aftercare

Protect young plants with horticultural fleece while they establish, and also later if unseasonal frost is forecast. Mulch around the plants with well-rotted compost in summer to help retain moisture in the soil; a moist growing medium is essential for the promotion of tuber development.

In late summer and early fall, the plants should be earthed up in the same way as potato crops, by drawing soil up around the base of the plants. This encourages stem rooting and the development of further tubers. Water during dry spells, especially in fall, when the tubers start to swell in response to shortening day length.

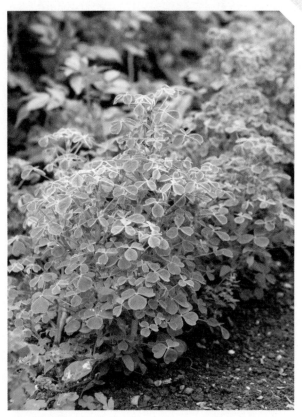

**The trefoil-shaped leaves** can also be picked and eaten in salads, but don't harvest too many or you will reduce the plants' ability to form tubers.

**Carefully uncover the tubers** with a fork or by hand and save a few for planting next spring.

## ④ Harvest

The longer the plants stay in the ground, the better. If early fall frosts are predicted, it's worth covering them with cloches or fleece to extend the growing season. Once foliage is blackened by frost, leave to die back completely for at least 2 weeks before harvesting the tubers. The sharp flavor of the flesh can be reduced by exposing tubers to sunlight for several days.

## Cook's tips

### Keep fresh
Tubers will keep until spring stored in breathable burlap or paper sacks in a light, cool, frost-free place.

### How to eat
Eat steamed, boiled, baked, or fried. Raw tubers are also delicious thinly sliced.

- Roast simply in a little oil and seasoning until tender.
- Dice cooked oca and combine with a vinaigrette dressing flavored with capers and sweet pickles for a twist on potato salad.
- The sharp taste of oca goes well with chile, and when finely sliced raw makes a crispy addition to a spicy Thai salad finished with lime.
- Scatter the sour-apple leaves in salads or use to garnish rich pork, duck, and fish dishes, and even desserts. Eat in moderation, though, due to the oxalic acid content.
- Harvesting in winter makes them an ideal addition to hearty soups, stews, and pies.

### How to preserve
Tubers store well, but can be frozen once cooked in soups and stews.

**Taro corms** are a type of modified underground stem and form just below the soil surface.

# Taro

*Level 3 advanced*

*Colocasia esculenta*

Unless you live in a tropical climate, cultivating taros for their sweet-potato-like corms can be a struggle. Gardeners in cooler climates need not despair, however, as they can still be grown for their beautiful "elephant ear" leaves, which are deliciously edible in their own right.

## What is it?

Taro is a perennial rainforest plant that evolved its large, slightly concave, heart-shaped leaves to help shed water from tropical downpours. The sweet, starchy corms are an important staple root crop in Southeast Asia and southern West Africa, and taro cultivation has a central place in Hawaiian culture. In the Caribbean, taro is mainly grown for its leaves, and is often used as the main ingredient in the vegetable stew "callaloo."

Taro has a claim to being one of the oldest food crops in the world, with evidence of cultivation dating back some 7,000 years.

**The species has fresh green** leaves and stems, but you can also buy cultivars with black stems and purple leaves.

## How do I grow it?

For corm cultivation, taros need long, hot summers; moderate to high humidity; and plenty of water. In the tropics, they are usually grown in soggy ground. In cooler climates, plants can be grown in a warm greenhouse for their edible leaves and are regularly successful outdoors, too. They grow in a range of soils from clay to deep, rich loam, and in small gardens can be grown in large containers of rich, moist potting mix. The easiest way to obtain corms for planting is to buy them from an Asian, West African, or Caribbean grocery shop. Otherwise, cultivars selected primarily for their ornamental foliage can be purchased from specialty nurseries.

Step-by-step growing »

## Quick guide

**Plant** when temperatures are high and the soil is warm

**Ideal range** 77–86°F (25–30°C); growth stops around 59°F (15°C)

**Grow** in rich soil in a warm, sheltered, sunny or partially shady spot

**Water** copiously with lukewarm water: it can't be overwatered!

**Plants grow** up to 3ft (1m) high and 3ft (1m) across

**Pick** a few young leaves from each plant; lift corms when the leaves die back

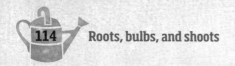

# Step-by-step growing

Taro is a tropical crop, so growth is faster in warm, humid conditions. In cooler climates, grow in a greenhouse or row covers, or as container plants for a sunny patio or a warm, bright spot in the house.

**When to grow and harvest**
Start into growth in early spring. Harvest young leaves in summer and the corms in fall.

| | early winter | late winter | early spring | late spring | early summer | late summer | early fall | late fall |
|---|---|---|---|---|---|---|---|---|
| break dormancy | | | ● | | | | | |
| plant | | | | ● | | | | |
| harvest | | | | | | ● | ● | ● |

## 1 Plant corms

Start plants under cover in early spring by planting corms in individual pots of moist growing mix. Place the pots in a warm greenhouse, or preferably in a propagator set to a temperature of around 86°F (30°C), or as warm as possible. Once the corm dormancy is broken, a new growing shoot will poke through the growing mix. Keep at a high temperature until the first set of leaf shoots emerges.

**Taro corms** have an obvious growing tip, and should be planted with the tip uppermost and only just covered by soil.

## 2 Transplant

Move the pots out of the heat and grow under cover, transferring to larger pots as they grow. Keep well watered using lukewarm water; a good trick is to keep the watering can in the greenhouse to warm for 24 hours before use.

Where temperatures remain above 59°F (15°C) throughout the growing season, young plants can be planted outdoors in late spring. Prepare the site by digging in plenty of organic matter and allow it to settle. Remove any weeds before planting and rake the soil to a rough level. Plants can also be moved to a growing bed in a warm greenhouse.

**Move plants** out of the heat needed to break dormancy once they show a pair of leaf shoots, but continue to grow under cover.

12-30in (30-75cm)

12-30in (30-75cm)

**Space plants** 12in (30cm) apart in warm but temperate climates, or 30in (75cm) apart if your climate is hot and humid.

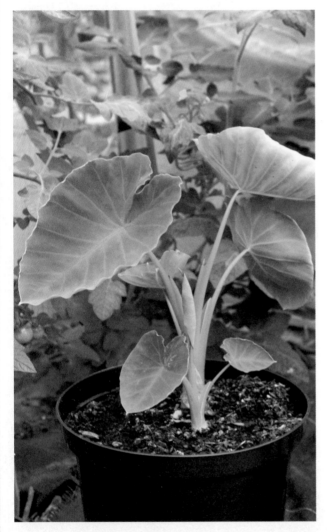

### ③ Growing in pots

Taro plants can be grown outdoors in summer in cooler climates by repotting them into large containers. Fill the containers with a 50:50 mix of multipurpose growing mix and garden soil, and place in a warm, sheltered, sunny location.

Taros can also be grown as houseplants, primarily for a harvest of edible leaves, in a warm bathroom, office, or conservatory. Mist plants with lukewarm water regularly where the air is dry, or set on a tray of pebbles filled with water. Grouping taro with other houseplants increases the humidity around the plant.

**The large**, heart-shaped leaves evolved to withstand tropical downpours and make taros appealingly architectural plants for pots.

### ④ Aftercare and harvest

However you grow your taros, keep them constantly moist, always watering with lukewarm water. Feed weekly with a liquid general fertilizer and also with a high-potash fertilizer 2 or 3 times per season.

Harvest young leaves as required, but not too many from a single plant. Withhold water before harvesting corms so the leaves die down. Lift when needed and store in a cool, dark place with good ventilation.

---

## Cook's tips

### Keep fresh
Once out of storage, use the corms quickly and don't keep them in the fridge, as they will rot if they get too cold.

### How to eat
Young leaves can be stuffed and steamed, while corms can be steamed, boiled, fried, stir-fried, roasted, baked, and braised. Wear rubber gloves to prepare the corms as they can irritate the skin.

- For traditional Hawaiian poi, steam until tender then purée with a little water and salt. Used as the basis for sweet and savory poi dishes.
- Cook chips by thinly slicing the corms, tossing in oil, and baking in the oven.
- Make a soup from both the corms and leaves, enriched with coconut cream.
- Mix boiled taro with a tomato masala sauce for the Indian vegetable dish *arbi ki sabji*.
- Use the leaves to make a Trinidadian version of callaloo stew with corned beef.

### How to preserve
Undamaged corms can be stored in a cool, dark, well-ventilated place for several months.

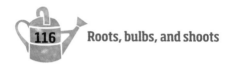

# Jicama

*Pachyrhizus erosus*

**Level 2** moderate

There is something slightly odd about sowing a bean to produce a root crop but, as all parts of the plant above ground are toxic, only the delicious crisp white flesh of the jicama tuber makes a suitable food crop. In fact, the seed pods contain the chemical rotenone, which is used as an insecticide.

## What is it?

The jicama is a perennial climber native to Mexico and is widely cultivated as an annual crop in Central America and Asia. It has many names over this range, including Mexican turnip, yam bean, and singkama. In these subtropical and tropical climates, the vigorous vine can grow to 16ft (5m) high, with blue or white flowers like sweet peas, followed by flat pods and huge tubers. More modest crops are possible in temperate climates with a frost-free growing season of 5 months.

### When to grow and harvest

Sow these tender plants early indoors and harvest as late as possible in fall.

| | early winter | late winter | early spring | late spring | early summer | late summer | early fall | late fall |
|---|---|---|---|---|---|---|---|---|
| sow indoors | | | ● | | | | | |
| plant out | | | | ● | ● | | | |
| harvest | | | | | | | ● | ● |

**Start plants off under cover** in spring to provide a long-enough growing season.

## How do I grow it?

Sow indoors, then plant outdoors or grow on in large containers in a greenhouse. Support the sprawling vines which, pruned to about 5ft (1.5m) high, make an attractive, fast-growing screen. Remove flowers to maximize tuber size.

### ① Sow indoors

Sow seed indoors 6 to 8 weeks before spring frosts are expected to finish. Soak in water for about 12 hours before planting to soften the seed coat and speed up germination. Sow in 3in (7.5cm) pots of moist potting mix, 2in (5cm) deep, and place on a warm windowsill or in a propagator at 68-73°F (20-23°C). Grow on until the last frost has passed. If roots peep through the bottom of the pots before this, transfer plants to larger pots.

### Keep fresh
Best eaten quickly. Keep in a cool, dark place, but not in the refrigerator.

### How to eat
Peel and eat raw in salads to taste its applelike flavor. The tuber is also cooked, usually in stir-fried dishes.

- Slice thinly and sprinkle with salt, lime juice, and chili sauce for a healthy Mexican snack.
- Substitute for water chestnuts in spring rolls.
- Add to soups, vegetable stews, or even pie fillings.

### How to store
Tubers can be kept for up to 2 months in a dry, dark place at 50–61°F (10–16°C). Large tubers store better.

## ② Plant on

Prepare soil by digging in well-rotted growing medium and covering with fleece to raise the temperature. Put cane supports in place. Harden plants off by moving them outdoors during the day and under cover at night for 2 weeks. Space plants 8in (20cm) apart, leaving at least 24in (60cm) between rows. If growing in a greenhouse, transplant to a border or move each plant into a large pot, with a diameter of at least 15in (38cm), filled with rich, all-purpose mix.

## ③ Aftercare and harvest

Usually free of pests and diseases in temperate regions, jicama grows rapidly in warm weather. Water outdoor plants generously in dry spells, and those in pots daily. Apply liquid tomato fertilizer weekly once flowering begins, and remove blooms and pinch back tips when they reach 3–5ft (1–1.5m) to encourage tuber formation. Tuber growth is linked to short days, so harvest as late as possible before the frost, covering with fleece on cold nights, if needed.

{ Level 1 easy }

# Earth chestnut

*Bunium bulbocastanum*

A truly multipurpose plant, the underground tubers, leaves, and seeds of the earth chestnut are all edible. While yields of the tubers may be modest, the rosettes of finely divided leaves and foamy clusters of white flowers are easily pretty enough to grace both productive and ornamental borders.

**Delicate, white, lacy flowers** start to bloom in early summer. The seeds are sometimes known as black cumin and can be harvested.

## What is it?

*Bunium bulbocastanum* is a relatively small, hardy, perennial plant found growing in grasslands throughout western and southern Europe, and is from the same family of plants as carrots and parsley. As its common name suggests, the flavor of the cooked tubers is similar to chestnut, while the raw leaves are akin to parsley and the seeds taste like a smokier version of cumin. With such a variety of culinary delights in one plant, the earth chestnut deserves to be far more widely cultivated. It shares a common name (and the name pignut) with the similar but larger *Conopodium majus*, which is also edible, so check the Latin name to avoid confusion.

## How do I grow it?

Seeds can be sown directly into the soil outdoors, but germination is more reliable when sown under cover. Young plants should then be grown on in pots and planted out once dormant in fall. Harvesting of leaves and seeds can begin in the second year, but the small tubers are slow to swell, making it best to begin harvesting them only at the end of the third growing season. In addition, plants often produce smaller baby tubers, which can be eaten or planted in fall and grown on. In the wild, earth chestnuts grow in chalky meadows and therefore do well in gardens with alkaline soil.

*The species name "bulbocastanum" gives away what's beneath the soil: a swollen root (bulbo) with the flavor of sweet chestnuts (castanum).*

**Tubers are** crisp and refreshing raw, turning sweet and chestnutlike when cooked.

## Quick guide

**Sow** under cover from early spring, or outdoors from late spring

**Minimum** 5°F (-15°C) to maximum 86°F (30°C)

**Grow** in moist, well-drained soil in sun or partial shade

**Water** after planting, then only in very dry weather

**Reaches** a height of 24in (60cm) and a spread of 10in (25cm)

**Harvest** tubers from fall, leaves from spring, and seeds from late summer

Step-by-step growing »

# Step-by-step growing

Earth chestnuts are tough plants that are easy to grow, but to harvest tubers you need to dig up entire specimens, and this means new plants must be propagated each year from seed or surplus tubers.

## When to grow and harvest

Sow in spring and grow on in pots before planting out when dormant in fall. Harvest from the second year.

| | early winter | late winter | early spring | late spring | early summer | late summer | early fall | late fall |
|---|---|---|---|---|---|---|---|---|
| sow indoors | | | ● | ● | | | | |
| sow outdoors | | | | ● | | | | |
| plant out | | | | | | | | ● |
| harvest tubers | ● | ● | | | | | | ● |
| harvest leaves | | | | | ● | ● | ● | |

**Give seed-raised plants** a full growing season in pots before planting out in fall.

## ① Sow seeds

In spring, sow seeds thinly in seed trays, cover with a thin layer of potting mix, water well, and place in a cold frame or greenhouse. Germination is usually within 14 days. Once the seedlings are large enough to handle, carefully prick them out individually into small pots. Continue growing them in their pots for the first summer, either in the cold frame or outdoors, keeping the potting mix moist but not waterlogged and transferring to larger pots as needed. Plant out, at least 12in (30cm) apart, once the leaves have died down in fall.

Seeds can be sown straight into the soil, but germination tends to be more erratic than those sown under cover. Where rows are required, sow generously into drills about 15in (38cm) apart. If the aim is a more natural drift of plants, scatter seed over the planting area. Either way, thin seedlings to 12in (30cm) apart when large enough to handle.

15in (38cm)

12in (30cm)

**Whether in rows** or drifts, space plants at intervals of 12in (30cm).

## ② Aftercare and harvest

Earth chestnuts rarely succumb to pest problems and are resilient plants, but if you want the tubers to swell as much as possible, ensure plants are kept watered during dry spells of weather. Plants are hardy and need no winter protection.

Only begin harvesting from the second year of growth. Leaves can be picked sparingly from late spring into fall, bearing in mind that it's the leaves that feed the swelling tubers. Seeds should ripen by late summer, when the whole heads can be cut and dried. Tubers are best lifted with a fork when the plants are dormant, from late fall through winter.

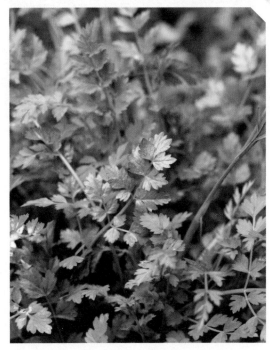

**The leaves look and taste** similar to flat-leaf parsley, but don't pick so many that the tubers suffer.

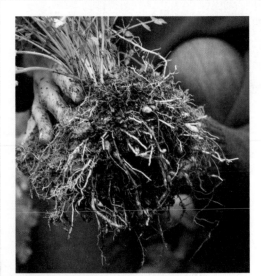

**Propagate new plants** by dividing a large, established clump into smaller sections.

## ③ Propagate

As harvesting the underground tubers requires lifting the whole plant, more will need to be planted for the supply to continue. Fortunately, earth chestnuts are easy to propagate, and you have a choice of methods. New plants can be raised from seed in spring using seed saved the previous summer. Any tubers that are too small for eating can also be planted in pots in spring and grown on for a season. Or if you leave a few plants to mature and bulk out, these can be lifted in spring or fall and carefully divided into several smaller plants, then replanted.

---

## Cook's tips

### Keep fresh

Eat leaves promptly after picking. Tubers keep for a few days in a cool, dark place, but begin to dry out pretty quickly.

### How to eat

Tubers can be eaten raw or cooked, while the leaves make a delicious herb, and the seeds an aromatic spice.

- The leaves can be used instead of parsley in any dish.
- The seeds are similar to cumin in flavor and are great for Indian-style curries, falafel, or Mexican black bean dishes.
- Thinly slice the crisp raw tubers and add to salads.
- Tubers become sweeter and more chestnutlike when cooked: enjoy them roasted in their skins or steamed and mashed with lots of cream and butter.

### How to preserve

When seed heads turn brown and papery, cut and hang them somewhere cool and dry for 2 weeks, then tap out the seeds. They will keep well in an airtight container for many months.

**Roots are ready** for harvesting once the first frosts of fall have killed the leaves.

# Skirret

*Sium sisarum*

**Level 2** moderate

This long-forgotten root vegetable was once highly prized in the 16th century and deserves a comeback. The taste is somewhere between a parsnip and a carrot, with a lingering peppery finish, and is best appreciated raw in salads or after gentle pan-frying.

## What is it?

Skirret is grown for its long, slender, swollen roots, which form a cluster at the base of the stem just below ground level. A native of Northern Europe and East Asia, skirret was first cultivated by the Romans, then regained popularity in medieval times, and was a mainstay of 16th-century cuisine in both sweet and savory dishes. With its dark, glossy leaves and tall spikes of lacy white flowers, which are highly attractive to bees and butterflies, skirret makes a wonderful addition to both the flower border and vegetable patch.

*The Roman emperor Tiberius was so fond of skirret, he demanded it as a tribute from vanquished German tribes of the Rhine.*

**Other root crops** can suffer a drop in yield if they run to flower, but skirret roots will keep on growing.

## How do I grow it?

Skirret is a very hardy perennial plant, and a single planting of just a few specimens will give you harvests for many years. You can either buy a crown of roots from specialty nurseries or raise them from seed, which can be sown under cover or directly outdoors once the soil has warmed. Germination can be erratic, so be sure to sow plenty of seeds. Skirret will thrive in most places but prefers damp, rich soil. It is found by streams in the wild and needs plenty of water, or the roots become woody. Provided you keep the plants weed free, they can be left to flower without any reduction in cropping.

## Quick guide

**Plant** crowns or sow seeds under cover from early spring

**Minimum** 14°F (-10°C) to maximum 77°F (25°C)

**Grow** in a sunny or partially shady spot in moist, rich soil

**Keep** well-watered: soil around the roots should never dry out

**Plants grow** up to 4ft (1.25m) in height and can spread to 24in (60cm)

**Harvest** roots in fall as needed or store in damp sand

**Step-by-step growing »**

# Step-by-step growing

Skirret can be grown by planting crowns or dormant roots in early spring, or by raising plants from seed. Grow in good, well-drained soil in a sunny position. Frequent watering will lead to tender, tasty roots.

### When to grow and harvest
Plant or sow from early spring for harvesting the following fall and winter.

| | early winter | late winter | early spring | late spring | early summer | late summer | early fall | late fall |
|---|---|---|---|---|---|---|---|---|
| sow indoors | | | ● | ● | | | | |
| sow outdoors | | | | ● | ● | | | |
| plant out | | | ● | ● | ● | | | |
| harvest | ● | ● | | | | | ● | ● |

## ① Prepare the soil

Choose a site in a sunny or partially shady area. Skirret prefers a rich, light, well-drained soil, so dig over the planting site and fork in plenty of well-rotted organic matter to enrich the soil and improve its structure. Allow 2–3 weeks before planting for the soil to settle. Rake the soil level, removing any weeds and large stones before planting.

**A rich, well-fertilized soil** will produce the best-quality crop for harvesting.

## ② Plant crowns or sow seeds

Plant crowns in spring as soon as possible after you get them. If the ground is frozen or waterlogged, they can be temporarily stored wrapped in damp cloth or burlap in a cool place. Plant crowns in rows 12in (30cm) apart, leaving the same distance between the crowns. Plant them so that the pinkish growing tips are level with the surface of the soil. Firm in the crowns, but avoid compacting the soil, then water in well.

Alternatively, sow seeds under cover in pots of garden soil from early to mid- or late spring. Germination takes between 6 and 20 days at 50–72°F (10–22°C). Grow on in a moderately cool place. Transplant the seedlings or sow seeds directly outdoors once the soil has warmed up enough, though germination can be erratic. Sow seeds ¾in (2cm) apart in drills 12in (30cm) apart, and thin out to a final spacing of 12in (30cm).

**Crowns** should be planted at soil level to prevent crown rot.

## ③ Aftercare

Keep plants well watered to prevent the roots becoming tough and inedible. Water before the onset of a spell of dry weather so that growth is not checked. Feed a liquid general fertilizer only if plants are lacking in vigor. Aphids can be a problem and should be removed by hand or tackled with an organic insecticide. Skirret self-seeds freely, but you can also collect the seeds by snapping off mature seed heads and storing them in a paper bag in a cool, dry place, until they dry out and shed their seeds.

**Aphids can be rubbed off** by hand if the infestation is light.

## ④ Harvest

Harvest from fall, once the tops have died back, by lifting the plants. Remove the best roots for eating and then select a few of the straightest, largest roots, without a woody core, for planting in spring the following year. Store roots in a layer of barely moist sand so they don't dry out. Alternatively, they are happy being left in the ground over winter until needed, though check that they are not being eaten by hungry rodents.

*Cook's tips*

### Keep fresh
When ready to eat, wrap the lifted roots in paper and store in the refrigerator.

### How to eat
Too delicate to peel, the roots need to be well scrubbed, especially if eating raw.

- Grate or finely slice and eat raw in a salad; goes well with spicy leaves such as arugula or watercress.
- Cube the roots and fry in butter with a little garlic.
- Combine parboiled skirret with grated apple, flour, and eggs to make fritters.
- Use instead of parsnips in a curried soup, or spiced with nutmeg and cinnamon.
- Finely slice and bake with cream for a seasonal gratin.

### How to preserve
Skirret roots will keep for several months before being transferred to the refrigerator for cooking and eating. Lift and store layered in boxes of damp sand in a cool shed or cellar. Alternatively, leave in the ground over winter and lift as needed, marking the spot with a cane so they can easily be found.

# Elephant garlic

*Allium ampeloprasum var. ampeloprasum*

**{ Level 1 easy }**

Given the right care and conditions, elephant garlic can produce truly gargantuan bulbs. Yet the cloves have a surprisingly subtle flavor that won't elephant-charge your taste buds: milder and sweeter than traditional garlic, they are ideal for roasting and baking.

## What is it?

Despite its name, elephant garlic is actually more closely related to leeks. The broad, flat leaves are a giveaway, as are the large, globe-shaped flowers borne on the end of tall, straight stems. In fact, the bright purple flowers are so pretty, you are most likely to find elephant garlic growing in the flower border alongside other ornamental alliums. Sadly, flowering is detrimental to bulb growth, and flower spikes should be broken off to direct the plants' energies into forming plate-busting bulbs. They need not be wasted, however, as the flower buds and stems (or "scapes") make a tasty early harvest in their own right.

> *Brought to the US by Balkan immigrants in the 1860s, elephant garlic was thought lost to cultivation until found growing wild in Oregon in the 1940s.*

**Cloves can be planted** directly outdoors or started off under cover in individual pots before being planted out.

## How do I grow it?

To grow elephant garlic, split off individual cloves from a bulb and plant them in rows. How early you plant the cloves is key to the kind of harvest you can expect. Planted early enough in the fall, the cloves will swell and then divide to produce large bulbs formed of multiple cloves. Planted in midwinter or later, they will form single bulbs and won't develop cloves. However, if you leave these later crops in the ground, they will continue to grow and divide the following year. Plants need to be kept well watered, but dislike waterlogging in winter. Try growing them on ridges or in raised beds if this is a problem. They also do not take kindly to competition, so you will need to keep the soil as weed-free as possible. Elephant garlic does not flourish on acidic soils. If you're not certain of your soil type, test it with a pH kit and fork in lime, if necessary.

Bulbs can grow to 8in (20cm) in diameter, weigh over 2¼lb (1kg), and produce cloves measuring 2 x 4in (5 x 10cm).

## Quick guide

**Plant cloves** in early to midfall, or late winter at the latest

**Minimum** 34°F (1°C) to maximum 86°F (30°C)

**Grow in** a sheltered, open, sunny site on free-draining soil

**Keep moist**, watering before the onset of dry weather, and stop 3 weeks before harvesting

**Rake** general fertilizer into the soil before planting

**Lift bulbs** when the leaves start to yellow

Step-by-step growing »

# Step-by-step growing

Each enormous clove can grow to at least the size of a normal bulb. To achieve such results, grow in light, free-draining soil in warm sunshine, provide plenty of moisture but prevent waterlogging, and keep weed free.

### When to grow and harvest
Plant in fall or spring, and harvest once the stems shrivel from mid- to late summer onward.

| | early winter | late winter | early spring | late spring | early summer | late summer | early fall | late fall |
|---|---|---|---|---|---|---|---|---|
| grow indoors | ● | ● | ● | | | | | |
| plant out | | | ● | ● | | | ● | ● |
| harvest | | | | | ● | ● | | |

## 1 Grow from cloves

If you are planting in their final positions outdoors in fall, split the bulb up into individual cloves and plant them with the narrow end uppermost, 1½in (4cm) deep and at the spacing described in step 2.

If you have missed the fall window, live in an area with cold winters, or if the planting site has a tendency to become waterlogged, it can be useful to start plants off under cover instead. Plant the cloves in medium pots in general potting mix.

**Place pots under cover** in a cool, bright location and keep the potting mix moist.

## 2 Plant out

Once plants started under cover have developed a good length of stem, and the soil has warmed up a little, plant them out 6in (15cm) apart and with 12in (30cm) between rows. Protect from birds with netting or horticultural fleece until established. They dislike competition, so keep the soil weed free. Weed by hand or use an onion hoe designed for weeding in tight spaces so as not to damage the developing bulbs.

**Gently tease out** the roots of plants started in pots before firming in their planting holes.

12in (30cm)

6in (15cm)

**Grow plants** at 6in (15cm) intervals with double the distance between rows.

## ③ Aftercare

Keep crops well watered, particularly before the onset of drought. Continue weeding regularly, removing the weeds at seedling or juvenile stage before they start to compete with the elephant garlic and rob the developing bulbs of moisture and nutrients.

## ④ Harvest

Harvest bulbs after the leaves have turned yellow and died back. Lift bulbs carefully, ease them from the ground with a trowel to avoid any damage, then rub off the soil or wash carefully and allow them to dry. They will store for at least 3 months provided they are not damaged or diseased, so inspect closely and discard or use immediately any suspect bulbs. Check stored bulbs regularly and use any that show signs of deterioration.

Leave any small but healthy plants in the ground and they will continue to grow the following year like a perennial, and the bulbs will divide into cloves and bulk up for harvest.

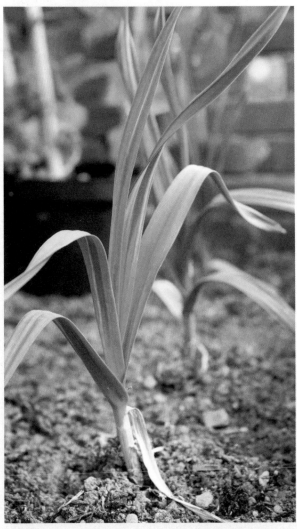

**Watch growing plants** for signs of flowering stems and cut any stems back by half to prevent them running to seed, which will diminish the size of the bulbs.

## Cook's tips

### Keep fresh
Store elephant garlic bulbs in a cool, dark, dry place with good air circulation. Do not refrigerate.

### How to eat
It is a great addition to a dish when a sweeter, subtle garlic flavor is needed.

- Roughly peel whole bulbs and drizzle olive oil inside, then wrap in foil and roast with seasonal vegetables.
- Gently fry chopped cloves as the base for a risotto or pasta sauce for a distinctive flavor.
- Make aioli sauce with puréed raw cloves–great with steak, grilled chicken, or roasted root vegetables.
- Add a smoky depth of flavor to creamy soups by stirring in the pulp of roasted cloves.

### How to preserve
Wrap whole, chopped, or crushed cloves in kitchen wrap or foil and place in a plastic bag in the freezer, breaking pieces off as needed. Freezing changes the flavor, however, and is not to everyone's liking.

{ } **Level 1** easy

# Daylilies
*Hemerocallis spp.*

Daylilies are easy to grow, and their gorgeous, exotic-looking flowers will brighten any garden. There are thousands of cultivars to choose from, all of them edible. The buds and open flowers are most commonly used in cooking, but the leaf stems, young shoots, and roots are edible, too.

## What is it?

Daylilies are perennial plants that grow for many years from special underground roots called rhizomes. Cultivated in China for centuries as medicinal and food plants, they are grown mainly as an ornamental plant in the West. Their trumpetlike flowers come in an impressive range of colors, from pale apricot to deep purple, and though each flower lasts for only a day, they are produced in abundance over a very long flowering season. The open flowers are the most nutritious, but they can be eaten at any time from bud to just-wilted bloom.

*Daylilies are mentioned in one of the earliest collections of Chinese folk songs, which dates back to the philosopher Confucius (551–479 BCE).*

**The unopened buds,** flowers, and wilted blooms can all be eaten and have a fresh flavor that is similar to green beans with a generous dash of spice.

## How do I grow it?

Daylilies look wonderful planted in groups in the flower border. Smaller, less vigorous varieties do well in pots, which can be positioned close to home to enjoy those that have a heady fragrance. Choose plants carefully, as late-flowering varieties are less likely to be attacked by the hemerocallis gall midge. The common orange daylily, *Hemerocallis fulva,* is the best all around for eating, with delicious young shoots and roots, as well as stunning, tawny-colored flowers. Daylilies are generally hardy but vary in their temperature tolerance, so check the label before buying. Plants grown in light shade produce fewer flowers, but the flowers last slightly longer than a day.

Step-by-step
growing ≫

## Quick guide

**Plant** container-grown plants any time of year, but preferably in spring

**Minimum** -22°F (-40°C) to maximum 86°F (30°C)

**Grow in** sun or light shade in fertile, moist, free-draining, neutral to slightly acidic soil

**Water well**, if needed, from spring until buds appear

**Size varies** between cultivars; some can reach 3ft (1m) in height and spread

**Pick flowers** as needed; harvest new shoots in spring and rhizomes in fall

**Most flowers open** from early morning, but nocturnal varieties open in the evening and last through the night.

# Step-by-step growing

Daylily blooms may not be long-lasting, but they are frequent and delicious. Plants can be raised from seed, grown from rhizomes, or bought as young plants from a nursery or garden center.

## When to grow and harvest
Container plants and those raised from rhizomes are best planted in spring or fall.

| | early winter | late winter | early spring | late spring | early summer | late summer | early fall | late fall |
|---|---|---|---|---|---|---|---|---|
| sow indoors | | | • | • | | | | |
| plant out | | | • | • | • | • | • | • |
| harvest | | | • | | | • | • | • |

## ① Sow indoors

Seeds need a period of cold before sowing to break dormancy. Put the seeds in damp sand in a freezer bag and put in the refrigerator at 39°F (4°C) for 6 weeks. Then in spring, sow seeds ½in (13mm) deep into moist, well-drained seed-starting mix kept at 55-68°F (13-20°C). Germination takes 21-49 days. When large enough to handle, transplant seedlings to 3in (8cm) pots and grow on. Harden off the young plants (see p.62) and plant them outdoors after the danger of frost has passed, or wait until the weather and soil warm up.

**Leave in pots** and do not plant out until the danger of frost has passed.

## ② Plant out

Before planting, prepare the ground by improving the soil with well-rotted organic matter, adding sharp sand and gypsum to clay soils for better structure and drainage, if necessary. Dig a planting hole slightly larger than the pot in which the daylily is planted, and scatter a root-booster of mycorrhizal fungi into the bottom of the planting hole. Remove the daylily from its pot, tease out the roots to encourage them to grow outward, and plant at the same depth that it was in the container.

**Clear all weeds** before planting to reduce competition for water and nutrients.

## Raising from rhizomes

Daylilies can also be grown from the bare rhizomes, which can be bought in packets from nurseries and garden centers. Only buy roots that are plump and show a few buds or small shoots. Plant them into pots of all-purpose mix, water well, and put them in a cold frame, in a cold greenhouse, or by a sheltered wall to bulk up. Always keep the medium moist. Transplant the plants into their final positions the following spring or fall.

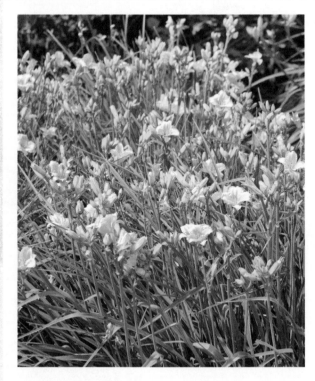

### ③ Aftercare and harvest

Mulch in spring with well-rotted organic matter, such as a homemade growing medium, manure, or leaf mold. If your plants lack vigor, feed them controlled-release fertilizer in spring to boost growth before mulching. Harvest buds and flowers as they appear in summer. Leaves taste better when they are emerging in early spring.

**All but the most** faded flowers are suitable for eating, and the more you pick, the more they bloom.

### ④ Dividing

Rejuvenate large, established clumps of daylilies by dividing them in fall or spring. Carefully dig the clump out of the ground and use two forks to ease the roots apart. Remove sections from the edge of the clump, 4–6in (10–15cm) in size, and replant these sections, leaving 12in (30cm) between each one.

**Dividing daylilies** provides a good opportunity to harvest some of the edible rhizomes.

## Cook's tips

### Keep fresh
Seal buds and flowers in a plastic bag and keep them in the vegetable drawer of the refrigerator.

### How to eat
Buds and flowers are used extensively in Asian cuisine, but the rhizomes and young shoots are edible, too.

- Strip the petals and use to add color to a salad.

- Sauté the buds in a little oil or butter and serve as a side dish.

- For a starter or tapas dish, dip buds and partly opened flowers in a light batter and deep-fry. Serve with a dipping sauce or sprinkled with salt.

- Use in a Chinese-style bone broth spiced with ginger.

- Young shoots have a mild taste of onion and can be cooked as a side dish or added to stir-fries.

- Smaller rhizomes taste a little like sweet potatoes and can be eaten raw, sautéed, or roasted.

### How to preserve
Buds and flowers can be dried in a dehydrator or an oven on very low heat, then rehydrated in hot water for 30 minutes before cooking.

# GRAINS
# AND SEEDS

**Amaranthus caudatus** is known for its bright, tassel-like flowers and pale green leaves. It thrives in a sunny spot.

# Amaranth

*Amaranthus caudatus*

**{ Level 1 easy }**

A combination of brightly colored leaves, stems, and flowers makes amaranth a very pretty crop to grow. Robust, vigorous, and productive, the plant has edible seeds packed with goodness and amino acids, making amaranth a superfood that is well worth growing.

## What is it?

Amaranth is a tall, upright plant that is easy to grow. From the top of the main stem erupts a prominent, pink, cascading flower head composed of numerous tassels, from which the edible seeds develop. Once a staple grain crop of the Incas, it was forgotten for centuries after the Spanish conquest, but has now been rediscovered in the West as a gluten-free grain rich in health-giving vitamins and minerals, ideal for making flat breads or using as popping "corn."

*Amaranth is a protein powerhouse: just a handful of seeds contains as much protein as a glass of milk.*

## How do I grow it?

As a spectacular, highly ornamental plant, amaranth is at home in both the flower border and the vegetable patch. Give it plenty of space, as it grows densely and shades surrounding plants, and in cooler climates amaranth will need shelter and plenty of sunshine. Seeds germinate easily and can be sown directly into the ground once the soil is warm or started off under cover. Amaranth can adapt to a wide range of soils, but growth is more compact, and it is more likely to flower and crop well in impoverished soils, even in poor summers. Grown to maximize cropping, its water requirements are low. If you are cultivating specimens primarily for their looks, however, give them rich soil and plenty of water; they will tend to flower later.

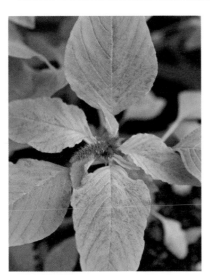

**The young leaves** can also be eaten much like spinach, though they have a sharper, slightly sweeter taste.

## Quick guide

**Sow** indoors, or directly outdoors once the soil has warmed

**Keep between** a minimum of 68°F (20°C) and a maximum of 86°F (30°C)

**Grow** in an open, sunny position in light, fertile, and free-draining soil

**Drought tolerant,** but water during dry conditions

**Plants grow** up to 2ft (60cm) tall

**Harvest** by shaking the flower heads, or strip away the grains into a bucket

**Step-by-step growing »**

# Step-by-step growing

Amaranth plants are easily raised from seed. If you have any spare seed left over, use it to grow nutty-tasting microgreens in a tray of potting mix placed on a sunny windowsill.

### When to grow and harvest
Sow in spring, harvest leaves as needed, and allow some plants to mature for harvesting seeds.

| | early winter | late winter | early spring | late spring | early summer | late summer | early fall | late fall |
|---|---|---|---|---|---|---|---|---|
| sow indoors | | | • | • | • | • | • | |
| sow outdoors | | | | • | • | | | |
| plant | | | | • | • | | | |
| harvest | | | | | • | • | • | • | • |

## 1 Sow seed

For early planting, sow indoors in modules to avoid seed disturbance, in a propagator, on a warm windowsill, or in a greenhouse at around 68°F (20°C). Transfer the seedlings carefully into larger pots as needed. Alternatively, once the soil is warm, sow the seed directly into finely raked soil. Either scatter the seed evenly in areas where it is to grow in groups, or sow it in rows in shallow drills, 8–12in (20–30cm) apart, then lightly cover it with soil, potting mix, or vermiculite.

**Amaranth grows rapidly,** going from seedling to mature plant in 10–12 weeks.

## 2 Transplant

Acclimatize indoor-sown plants to the colder temperatures outside by placing them in a cloche or cold frame and gradually increasing ventilation first during the day and then also at night. Once all danger of frost has passed, transplant the young plants into their final positions. Choose a sunny, sheltered location in free-draining soil; add a little grit to improve drainage if needed, and clear the site of weeds. In cooler climates, crops can be grown in a border within a greenhouse or in a hoophouse. Space plants at intervals of 12–16in (30–40cm) in rows 8–12in (20–30cm) apart. Good spacing is important for helping to minimize the risk of downy mildew.

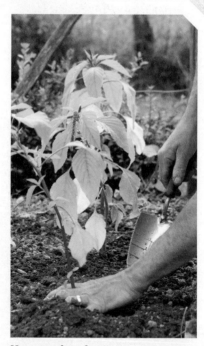

**Use your hand** to firm the soil around the stem, then water the plants in well.

8–12in (20–30cm)

12–16in (30–40cm)

**Leave plenty** of space between plants so that they do not shade their neighbors.

# ③ Aftercare

Keep the plants weed-free and water in periods of drought. Apply a mulch around the base of the plants to retain moisture and warmth. Pinch back the growing tips when 8in (20cm) tall to promote bushiness. Feed a diluted liquid tomato fertilizer every 2–3 weeks to encourage flowering.

**Support plants**, if necessary, by tying them into sturdy stakes or canes.

# ④ Harvest

After approximately 3 months of growth, the plants should be mature and the seeds ready to harvest. Seeds fall freely when they are ripe, and just a light nudge of the flowering tassels will dislodge them. Harvest them on a dry day by bending the flower stem slowly over a clean bucket, and then vigorously shaking or rubbing the seed heads together. Finally, remove the chaff by spreading through a fine sieve, and leave the seeds on a tray to dry.

**Remove the chaff** to reveal the seeds, which are red here, but they also come in white, beige, or black.

**The deep red flowers** that bloom in the summer make amaranth ideal ornamental, as well as edible, plants.

## Cook's tips

### Keep fresh

Eat leaves fresh, or store in a sealed plastic bag, or wrapped in paper towel in the vegetable drawer of the refrigerator for a few days.

### How to eat

Seeds can be eaten as a breakfast cereal; put in hot oil; mixed with grains; or added to soups, stews, and stir-fries. Leaves can be steamed or eaten raw in salads; young stems can be cooked.

- To use amaranth as a cooked "grain," cover with water, bring to a boil, and simmer for approximately 20 minutes.
- Use the cooked grain instead of tabbouleh in a herby salad.
- The cooked seeds make a creamy oatmeal: just heat in milk and add nuts and fruit.
- Give dairy desserts a light crunch with popped amaranth.
- Fry leaves and steamed stems with garlic, cumin, and chilies for a light side dish.

### How to preserve

Dried seed lasts for months in an airtight container stored in a cool, dark, dry place.

## Quick guide

**Sow** under cover in spring and transplant or sow outdoors once the soil is warm

**Minimum** 64°F (18°C) to maximum 90°F (32°C)

**Grow** in full sun; it is tolerant of most soils, though productivity is best in neutral soil

**Only water** during severe drought

**Plants grow** up to 6½ft (2m) in height and 12in (30cm) in spread

**Harvest** in fall, when seeds are dry

{ Level 1 easy } # Quinoa
*Chenopodium quinoa*

Quinoa (pronounced "keen-wa") is a cereal crop with a range of colored seed heads, which vary from green to deep red, according to the variety. It is easy to grow, tolerant of the cold, and highly nutritious. Seeds can be boiled as an alternative to rice or ground into a gluten-free flour, and the leaves are edible, too.

## What is it?

Quinoa is a fast-growing annual in the same family of plants as amaranth, spinach, and lamb's quarters. Also known as Inca wheat, it was first cultivated as a crop by the Incas of Peru, and to signify the start of the growing season the Inca Emperor would plant the first sacred seeds with a golden spade. Nearly 500 years later, it is esteemed once again by dietitians and foodies as a superfood with a full complement of amino acids, which makes it an excellent vegan source of complete protein.

### When to grow and harvest

Start sowing in early spring and harvest from late summer when the seeds have matured.

| | early winter | late winter | early spring | late spring | early summer | late summer | early fall | late fall |
|---|---|---|---|---|---|---|---|---|
| sow indoors | | | • | • | • | | | |
| sow outdoors | | | | • | • | | | |
| plant out | | | | • | • | | | |
| harvest | | | | | | | • | • |

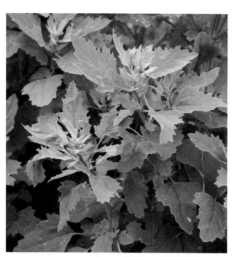

**Pick tender young leaves** for eating raw in salads; the tougher, older leaves can be cooked and eaten like spinach.

## How do I grow it?

Quinoa is straightforward to grow and germinates easily. Sow early if growing for seeds, as later sowings will provide only a harvest of leaves. If your growing season is short, feed plants tomato fertilizer to stimulate flower production.

### ① Prepare the soil

Rich, free-draining soils produce the highest yields, so improve the soil a few weeks in advance of sowing or planting out by digging in plenty of well-rotted organic matter. Don't overdo it, however, or plants may produce leafy growth at the expense of seeds. Allow the ground to settle, and make sure the soil is clear of all weeds; if sowing directly outdoors, rake the soil into a fine seedbed.

## Cook's tips

### Keep fresh
Store dry seed in an airtight container in a cool, dark place.

### How to eat
Seeds must be boiled for 10-15 minutes before they are ready to eat. Enjoy it as a substitute for rice or as a gluten-free alternative to pasta, couscous, and bulgur.

- Give soups a nutrient boost by adding dry quinoa before pouring in the stock.
- Mix with mashed beans, eggs, and herbs and spices to make a veggie burger.
- Stir through roast vegetables and top with a tahini sauce.

### How to preserve
Dry seeds can last 3 years in an airtight container.

## ② Grow from seed

Sow under cover in small pots placed in a propagator set at 64-75°F (18-24°C), sowing ¼in (5mm) deep in seed-starting mix. Harden off seedlings (see p.62), then transplant outdoors after the last frosts, leaving 14in (35cm) between plants and at least 24in (60cm) between rows. You can also sow directly outdoors once the soil has warmed. High temperatures can induce dormancy, however, and if this is the case, shade the soil, sow in the evening, or water before sowing.

## ③ Aftercare and harvest

Keep plants well watered and free of weeds, and provide support if needed. Harvest on a sunny day after the seeds turn yellow and start to fall. Cut off the seed heads carefully, leaving a bit of stem as a handle, and dry them on trays or in a paper bag in a warm, dry place. After 2 weeks, rub the seed heads so the seeds fall, and pass through a fine sieve. Just before using, rinse the seeds in water to wash off the bitter taste they produce to deter predators.

{ Level 1 easy }

# Chia

*Salvia hispanica*

Chia, once a lost crop of the Aztecs, is now a plant with a top billing. The seeds contain more omega-3 fatty acids than salmon, a wealth of antioxidants, minerals, a complete source of protein, and more fiber than flaxseeds. Dubbed "the ultimate superfood" by advocates, athletes, and ultra-runners, now it's your turn to feel the power!

## What is it?

Chia seeds are harvested from the plant *Salvia hispanica*, a tall, upright annual with bright green leaves and spikes of blue flowers that appear in summer. It is native to southern Mexico and Guatemala, and the Aztecs and Mayans are believed to have relied heavily on chia seeds as sustenance during hunting and harvesting periods. Plants need a hot, sunny position and a long summer to give enough time for the seeds to mature.

*Chia is a species in the Salvia genus, which also includes the herb sage and as many as 900 ornamental flowering plants.*

**Harvest the seeds** by gathering the flowering spikes once the flowers are over and the seed heads have dried.

## How do I grow it?

Chia plants are best raised from seed sown early indoors, unless your climate is warm enough to sow directly outdoors from early spring. Plants need moisture-retentive, moderately fertile, free-draining, light soil, and a position in full sun where the soil will warm up quickly in spring. The light blue flowers would make a valuable addition to an ornamental flower border. Plants also grow well in containers of gritty potting mix, making it ideal for a patio or balcony. If possible, grow plants in a sheltered position near a wall to take advantage of radiated heat.

**Chia bears** attractive blue flowers in upright spikes, but only once there are fewer than 12 hours of daylight.

## Quick guide

**Sow** seeds indoors in spring and transplant when there is no danger of frost

**Minimum** 52°F (11°C) to maximum 96.8°F (36°C)

**Grow** in a sheltered, sunny position on free-draining soil

**Keep moist** to slightly dry; do not overwater

**Plants reach** 4ft (1.2m) high and 16in (40cm) across

**Gather** the mature seed heads from summer until fall

Step-by-step growing »

# Step-by-step growing

Start chia plants off under cover and plant out in a sunny spot in light, fertile soil. Keep the soil moist, but never waterlogged, and pinch back shoots to encourage branching.

**When to grow and harvest**

Sown early enough and with a warm fall, plants in cooler, northerly climates may set seed; otherwise, grow for leaves.

| | early winter | late winter | early spring | late spring | early summer | late summer | early fall | late fall |
|---|---|---|---|---|---|---|---|---|
| sow indoors | | | ● | ● | | | | |
| sow outdoors | | | | ● | | | | |
| plant out | | | | ● | | | | |
| harvest | | | | | ● | ● | ● | ● |

## 1 Sow indoors

Sow indoors in spring, about a month before the frosts end in your area. Sow the tiny seeds into moist seed-starting mix and lightly cover by sieving over a fine layer of potting mix or vermiculite. Place in a warm greenhouse or propagator set to 70–77°F (21–25°C) until germinated. Keep the potting mix moist and transplant the strongest seedlings into individual pots of loam-based or all-purpose mix. Continue growing under cover, potting up to larger pots as needed. Seedlings are ready for planting out when they are 3–4in (8–10cm) tall.

**Chia seeds germinate** in about 7 days and can be transplanted with the aid of a dibble when large enough to handle.

## 2 Plant out

Once all risk of frost has passed, harden off the young plants for a week or so by placing them outdoors during the day and returning them to shelter at night. Alternatively, transfer the plants to a cold frame and prop the lid open during the day, shutting it again at night. Once acclimatized, plant out at 24in (60cm) intervals in rows 36in (90cm) apart.

You can also directly sow seeds outside after the last frosts and when the soil has warmed enough. Sow into a raked-over seedbed, either in drills or broadcast, and sow more than you need. Lightly cover, keep moist, and progressively thin out until you are left with the strongest plants 24in (60cm) apart.

**Transfer acclimatized** plants to a sunny location outdoors.

36in (90cm)

24in (60cm)

**Chia plants** grow tall and bushy, and need plenty of space around them.

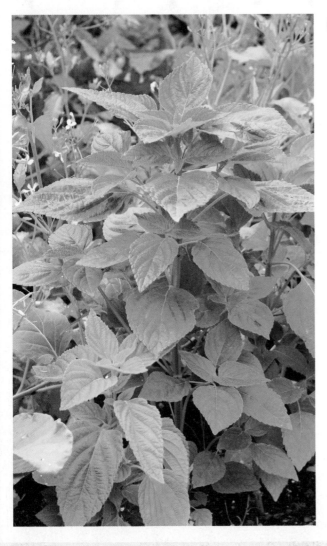

**Plants can grow** as tall as 6ft (2m), and on windy sites may need tying in to stakes or canes for support.

## ③ Aftercare

Chia doesn't like competition for water and nutrients, so keep on top of the weeding until plants are established, and water regularly. It is worth applying a thick mulch of well-rotted organic matter to suppress weeds and help lock in moisture.

Chia plants have a tendency to grow tall and leggy, but you can prevent this by pinching back the tips to encourage branching and bushier growth. When a plant has produced 4 leaves, pinch back the growing tip just above a leaf. This causes sideshoots to form, which should then be pinched back once they have produced 3–4 leaves.

## ④ Harvest

Harvest seeds by gathering flower spikes when most of the petals have fallen. Place in open paper bags and leave in a warm, airy place to dry out. Crush the dried seed heads to release the seeds and sieve out the chaff. Chia is a short-day plant and needs fewer than 12 hours of daylight to initiate flower and seed production. In cooler northerly climates, short days come too late in the season, and plants are frosted before seeds can be set. You can, however, gather the leaves throughout the growing season to make infusions.

### Cook's tips

**Keep fresh**

Store seeds in an airtight container in a cool, dark, dry place. Fresh leaves are best used immediately.

**How to eat**

Dry seeds can be added to baked goods or scattered over any number of dishes for a crunchy nutrient boost. Soaked in liquid, the seeds swell and take on a goopy texture that works well in desserts and oatmeal.

- Use in place of poppy seeds in recipes for cakes, loaves, flat breads, and crackers.
- Stir a tablespoon into a few handfuls of oats and leave to soak in milk overnight for an extra-creamy bowl of cereal in the morning.
- Add soaked seeds to milky or creamy desserts, such as rice pudding.
- Pour boiling water over chopped fresh or dried leaves for an invigorating tea.

**How to preserve**

Seeds can last for 5 years stored as described above. Chopped leaves can be dried in a dehydrator or very low oven and used for tea.

# Sesame

*Sesamum indicum*

You may be surprised to discover that the seeds found on top of a burger bun come from a highly ornamental plant bearing flowers very similar in appearance to a foxglove. Once pollinated, the flowers develop into green, torpedo-shaped pods containing the nutritious seeds that are so high in cholesterol-lowering "good" fats.

## Quick guide

**Sow** indoors, harden off carefully, and plant out only once the last frost has passed

**Minimum** 73°F (23°C) to maximum 86°F (30°C)

**Sesame** will flourish in warm, moist, free-draining soil

**Water** when soil or medium is dry, but do not overwater

**Plants grow** up to 35in (90cm) tall and spread to 20in (90cm)

**Harvest** when pods turn brown, just before the seeds are shed

## What is it?

A tall, upright, annual plant native to tropical India, sesame bears elongated oval leaves and attractive pink or white flowers that grow in threes at the junction of the main and leaf stems. Seeds range in color from cream to black or red, and can be eaten whole or crushed for their oil. The seeds have been munched for centuries; records exist on ancient Assyrian tablets and in the writings of Marco Polo of sesame being grown as a crop, long before burgers were invented.

### When to grow and harvest

Sow indoors in spring and plant out when soil and weather are warm. Harvest from late summer, depending on climate.

| | early winter | late winter | early spring | late spring | early summer | late summer | early fall | late fall |
|---|---|---|---|---|---|---|---|---|
| sow indoors | | | • | • | | | | |
| sow outdoors | | | | • | • | | | |
| plant out | | | | | • | | | |
| harvest | | | | | | | • | • |

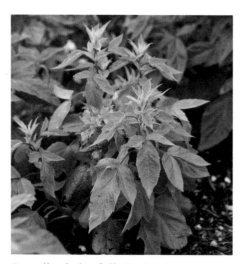

**As well as being full** of healthy fats, sesame seeds are also high in fiber, metabolism-boosting vitamin B1, and an assortment of minerals.

## How do I grow it?

Sesame is a warm-climate crop but can be grown outdoors in temperate areas with long, hot summers, or raised in the greenhouse. Grow in a sheltered, sunny spot, ideally close to a sunny wall to benefit from the radiated heat.

## ① Sow indoors

Sow indoors 6 weeks before the last frost, ½in (1cm) deep in modules or trays of moist, well-drained seed-starting mix, covered to block out the light. Keep in a propagator heated to 72–77°F (22–25°C) and mist the potting mix with lukewarm water to maintain dampness. Germination takes 7–14 days. Remove the cover as soon as the seedlings emerge and place in a sunny spot or windowsill. Water lightly with lukewarm water when the medium is dry.

## Cook's tips

### Keep fresh

Dry seeds thoroughly and store in an airtight jar in a cool, dark place.

### How to eat

Use whole seeds raw or toasted, or grind to a paste. Thinnings can also be used as a microgreen.

- Make tahini by grinding the seeds with a little oil.
- Toast seeds in a dry frying pan and sprinkle over salads, fish dishes, or roasted vegetables.
- Stir into a pancake mix or use as a topping for bread.

### How to preserve

Double-bag seeds before freezing to avoid flavor taint from other foods.

## ② Plant and sow outdoors

Harden off carefully (see p.62) and plant out at least 2 weeks after the last frost, spacing plants 6–8in (15–20cm) apart. You can also sow directly outdoors at this point. Sow in drills and sow more than you need, thinning plants to 6–8in (15–20cm) apart. Plants can also be grown on in containers filled with all-purpose mix.

## ③ Aftercare and harvest

Sesame is very drought tolerant; keep the soil moist, erring on the dry side, but never waterlogged. Plants grown in cooler climates will benefit from a feed of high-potassium fertilizer. The seed pods form inside the fading flowers. Harvest as the pods start to dry out and before they split. Leave on a tray in a warm, airy place to dry, then gently crack open the pods and remove the seeds.

{ **Level 2** moderate }

# Strawberry popcorn

*Zea mays Everta Group*

This popping variety of maize bears ruby-red kernels on miniature cobs that can be popped whole and the popcorn eaten straight from the husk–popcorn-on-the-cob, anyone? If that doesn't appeal, the dried cobs make pretty decorations.

## What is it?

Maize or corn is an annual plant belonging to the same family of grasses as wheat and lawn grass. Popping corn is the same species as sweetcorn, but comes from the Everta Group selected for the hard outer hulls to their kernels, which rupture explosively when the starch inside is heated to a sufficient degree. Evidence for the sale of popping corn dates back to the 1820s, and by 1848, the word "popcorn" had appeared in the dictionary.

*Although humans have been popping corn for over 3,000 years, the first commercial popcorn machine was invented in Chicago in 1885.*

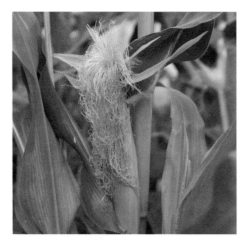

**Known as "silks,"** the female flowers grow from the ears of the plant and catch pollen produced by the male flowers at the top.

## How do I grow it?

This variety only grows to 4ft (1.25m) tall and is ideal for growing in a small garden or containers. To do well, strawberry popcorn needs a long, warm growing season and moisture-retentive, free-draining soil. Dig in plenty of well-rotted organic matter where you are going to plant, or use ground that has been improved for a previous crop. It is also helpful to warm the soil where you are going to grow your crops by laying black plastic over it for a few weeks before planting out. If you have space or are simply a big fan of popcorn, make repeat sowings every 2 weeks until midsummer to extend the harvesting season. Watering is particularly beneficial at the point when plants begin to flower, and then again as the grains start to swell.

**Individual cobs** of strawberry popcorn grow to around 4–6in (10–15cm) in length–much smaller than cobs of regular corn.

Step-by-step growing »

# Step-by-step growing

Sow indoors to extend the season, or outdoors once the soil is warm. Plant in blocks, not rows, and leave pollination to nature, or help by giving plants a gentle shake.

## When to grow and harvest

Sow from late winter and harvest from early summer, depending on the weather.

| | early winter | late winter | early spring | late spring | early summer | late summer | early fall | late fall |
|---|---|---|---|---|---|---|---|---|
| sow indoors | | ● | ● | | | | | |
| sow outdoors | | | | ● | ● | | | |
| plant out | | | | ● | ● | | | |
| harvest | | | | | ● | ● | ● | |

## 1 Sow indoors

Sow a pair of seeds 1–1½in (2.5–4cm) deep in 3in (7.5cm) pots or modules of moist seed-starting mix. Place on a sunny windowsill, in a greenhouse, or in a propagator set to 68–79°F (20–26°C). Once germinated, thin carefully to leave the strongest seedling. Plants are sensitive to root damage and disturbance, so do this while they are still small and use a trowel or dibble to help you. Once all risk of frost has passed, harden off the young plants to outdoor conditions for a week or so, placing them outside during the day and returning them to shelter at night. Alternatively, transfer to a cold frame and prop the lid open during the day, before shutting it again at night.

**The seeds are a favorite** food of mice, so it is best to protect exposed pots or trays, especially if growing in a greenhouse.

## 2 Plant out

Once acclimatized, move the young plants to their final growing positions outdoors. Plant 15in (38cm) apart, in rows 18in (45cm) apart.

Strawberry popcorn plants are short for corn, rising to only 4ft (1.25m) tall, which makes them suitable for growing in containers. Fill the pots with potting mix, keep plants well-watered, and feed them liquid general fertilizer regularly until established, then change to a high-potassium fertilizer, such as tomato feed.

Seeds can also be sown in situ at around this time. Sow 2 or 3 seeds under cloches or jars at the final spacing, and thin to leave the strongest seedling. You may need to net the sowing area against mice until the seedlings establish.

**Plant out** the young plants before they start to get pot-bound.

18in (45cm)

15in (38cm)

**Plant in rectangular blocks** rather than long rows, so the pollen has the best chance of being blown on to neighboring crops.

# ③ Aftercare

Protect the young plants with cloches or windbreaks if the weather turns cold. Remove weeds between plants, but take care not to damage roots growing near the soil surface. Keep plants well watered when the flowers appear, then again when the cobs are developing, and if there is a spell of drought in the meantime. In windy sites, plants may also need earthing up or staking as they grow tall.

Corn is naturally wind-pollinated, but you can provide a helping hand. When the male flowers at the top of the plant start releasing pollen, you will notice clouds of yellow dust on the lower leaves or when you brush against the plants. Give the stem of each plant a gentle shake to encourage pollen to drop from these male flowers to the silky tassels of the female flowers emerging from the juvenile cobs below. Do this every day until no more pollen is released.

**Keep plants well-watered** until they establish and in periods of drought. Provide additional watering when the flowers appear and cobs begin to form.

# ④ Harvest

Harvest when the tassels on the cobs have darkened. Since they are popped rather than eaten as corn on the cob, any lack of sweetness isn't the end of the world, and it doesn't matter if you pick them a bit early. At this point, cut the cobs and some stalk and gently remove the outer husk and tassel debris. Hang the picked cobs in a dry, airy place until you're ready to pop them.

**Plants sown indoors** should be ready for picking by early to midsummer.

---

## Cook's tips

### Keep fresh

Store in a sealed container, but do not keep in the refrigerator, as this can dry out the kernels.

### How to eat

Cook them for popping corn. You could leave the cobs to dry out and use them in a decorative display, but this seems a terrible waste! Carefully remove the kernels with a sharp knife, or pop whole cobs at a time.

- Method 1–Pour enough oil to cover the bottom of a lidded saucepan. Place on medium heat and add the kernels when the oil is sizzling. Put the lid on quickly and keep agitating to avoid burning the kernels. Lift the lid when the popping stops.

- Method 2–Place cob in a large paper bag and microwave on high heat for 4-5 minutes.

- Enjoy the popcorn plain, tossed with salt and melted butter, or flavor as desired.

### How to preserve

Store cobs and kernels in a sealed container in a cool, dark, dry place, such as a garage, shed, or similar area. Do not allow to dry out if using for popcorn.

# HERBS AND SPICES

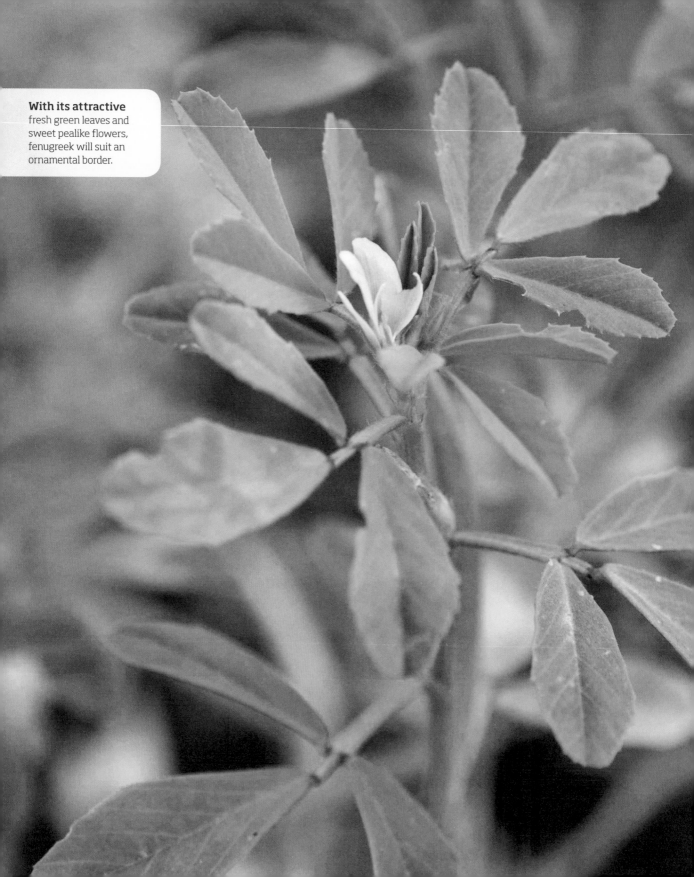

**With its attractive** fresh green leaves and sweet pealike flowers, fenugreek will suit an ornamental border.

**Level 1** *easy*

# Fenugreek

*Trigonella foenum-graecum*

Fenugreek is often sown for its nitrogen-fixing abilities as a green manure, but it is well worth growing as a food crop to harvest its pungent, earthy leaves, which are used fresh or dried in many Indian dishes. Allow a few plants to flower and pod for a second harvest of spicy seeds.

## What is it?

Fenugreek is an easy-to-grow annual in the same family of plants as peas and beans, with pretty, oval-shaped leaves that grow in sets of three like clover. There are two forms: a large-seeded variety with white flowers, which can only be cut once; and a smaller-seeded variety with slightly smaller leaves and yellow flowers, which will regrow after cutting. Plants produce long, thin, green seed pods like curved beaks, which turn yellow when ripe. Both leaves and seeds are rich in nutrients and fiber, and are reputed to help relieve digestive problems and lower blood sugar levels.

*"Fenugreek" comes from the Latin for "Greek hay," probably because the plant was first cultivated in the Near East and the dried leaves smell a little like hay.*

**Sow seeds outdoors** in a fine seedbed. Germination is usually rapid and reliable.

## How do I grow it?

Plants have a degree of frost resistance and can be sown outdoors from early spring until well into fall. Grow in a sunny, sheltered, well-drained position on light, moist, free-draining soil. Fenugreek is a useful crop for growing in small gardens, as it doesn't need much space. Plants also do well in containers filled with all-purpose mix. If growing the larger variety for its leaves rather than seeds, make repeat sowings, as it does not regrow after being cut. The smaller-seeded variety can be grown as a cut-and-come-again crop. Seeds can also be sprouted and grown for microgreens.

## Quick guide

**Sow** indoors from late winter and outdoors from early spring to early fall

**Minimum** 32°F (0°C) to maximum 90°F (32°C)

**Choose** a sheltered, sunny spot on light, free-draining soil

**Not a thirsty** crop, but don't let the soil dry out

**Grows to** 24in (60cm) in height and 16in (40cm) in spread

**Harvest** leaves once plants are established; leave a few plants to grow on for seeds

**Step-by-step growing »**

# Step-by-step growing

Grow in light, well-drained soil in a sunny position. Fenugreek does not have a high demand for water, but growth will be more rapid if the soil is kept moderately moist. Protect from pigeons until established.

## When to grow and harvest

Make successional sowings throughout the season, especially if you are growing the large-leaved variety for its leaves.

|  | early winter | late winter | early spring | late spring | early summer | late summer | early fall | late fall |
|---|---|---|---|---|---|---|---|---|
| sow indoors |  | ● | ● |  |  |  |  |  |
| transplant |  |  | ● | ● |  |  |  |  |
| sow outdoors |  |  | ● | ● | ● | ● | ● |  |
| harvest |  |  |  |  | ● | ● | ● | ● |

## 1 Sow indoors

If you want an early crop, start plants off indoors in late winter. Fenugreek can get unhappy about being transplanted, so grow the seedlings in modules to minimize root disturbance. Germination is rapid and usually takes less than a week. Carefully pot up the seedlings to individual pots before they start to outgrow their modules. Fenugreek withstands spells at 32°F (0°C), but it is best to wait until after the last frosts before hardening off (see p.62) and planting out indoor-raised seedlings.

**Sow a single seed** to each module so that you do not disturb the roots by thinning out.

## 2 Plant and sow outdoors

Improve the structure and nutrients at the growing site by digging in well-rotted organic matter, and allow to settle. Transplant seedlings 2in (5cm) apart in rows 8in (20cm) apart. To sow direct, rake the soil to a fine texture and form drills ¼in (0.5cm) deep. Sow seeds thickly and cover lightly. Once seedlings emerge, thin plants to 2in (5cm) apart. Repeat-sow seeds of the large-leaved variety once a row has germinated, as it does not regrow after flowering.

**Keep the soil** around seedlings and young plants free of weeds to help them establish.

8in (20cm)

2in (5cm)

**Fenugreek plants** don't suffer from being grown close together, and the proximity helps to smother weeds.

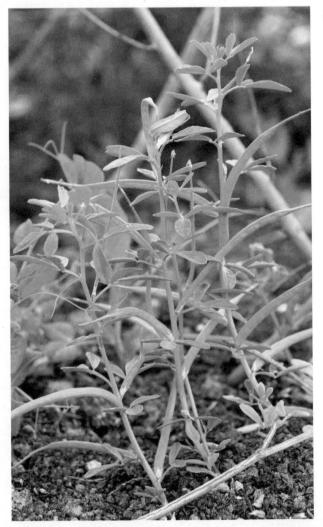

## 3 Aftercare and harvest

Cover seedlings and young plants with netting or horticultural fleece to prevent them from being eaten by pigeons. Carefully hoe or remove weeds by hand until plants have established themselves, after which rapid growth acts as a weed-suppressant. Water only if the soil looks dry. Harvest leaves from 6 weeks after sowing, when plants are 10in (25cm) tall or less, and before flowers appear, after which the quality deteriorates. Cut stems just above soil level. The small-leaved variety can be cut several times to keep it productive and prevent seeding.

**Leave some plants** to flower and produce seed pods for a second harvest of seeds.

## 4 Harvesting seeds

If growing plants for seeds, you can remove some leaves, but not so many to weaken growth. Harvest the pods once they have turned yellow but before they split. If the pods are wet, dry the seeds on a tray before storing.

**Try to harvest** after a spell of sunny weather so the seeds will be dry.

## Cook's tips

### Keep fresh

Store fresh leaves in a plastic bag in the refrigerator for 2–3 days. Plunge in cold water for 30 minutes to refresh wilted leaves.

### How to eat

Fresh leaves can be used as a substitute for watercress in salads or lightly cooked and eaten like spinach. Both fresh and dried fenugreek are widely used in Indian cuisine. Look out for recipes with *methi* in the title, which is Hindi for fenugreek.

- Combine with potatoes in the classic Punjabi dish aloo methi.
- Dried leaves are one of the key flavorings for Old Delhi-style butter chicken.
- Stir fresh or dried leaves into dough to flavor flat breads.
- Make a lahmajoun (Armenian pizza) spiced with ground fenugreek and cumin seeds.
- Sprinkle the seeds whole on vegetables to roast.

### How to preserve

Dry leaves slowly on trays in an oven on very low heat. Leaves and seeds will keep for one year in airtight containers in a cool, dry place.

{ } **Level 1** *easy*

# Wood sorrel

*Oxalis acetosella* or *O. violacea*

This diminutive perennial plant, with its fresh, green, cloverlike leaves and dainty white spring flowers, is a beautiful addition to gardens with dappled shade. With high levels of oxalic acid, the foliage should not be consumed in large quantities, but as a garnish it is prized for its wonderful sour-apple flavor.

## What is it?

Wood sorrel is a common name applied to many species of *Oxalis*, but the delicate native species of moist woodlands are *Oxalis acetosella* throughout Europe and Central Asia, and *Oxalis violacea* in North America. The trefoil-shaped leaves are thought to be the original shamrock, and are sent up from small rhizomes to form spreading carpets among the leaf litter. They have been a popular plant with foragers for centuries, but, though easy to grow, are not commonly found in gardens. Stock is often available from wildflower nurseries, or plants can be collected from the wild with the landowner's permission.

> Another common name for wood sorrel is "Alleluia," so called because the flowers appear between Easter and Pentecost.

**The delicate flowers** and soft green leaves of wood sorrel open up during the day, then fold up at night to protect themselves from harsh weather.

## How do I grow it?

Although wood sorrel is extremely hardy, it is best propagated in the light shade and shelter of a cold frame. This can be done successfully in three ways: by sowing seeds in spring, by planting dormant rhizomes in fall, or by lifting and dividing existing clumps in spring. Grow in a moist but free-draining site, and enrich the soil with leaf mold before planting out. Once established in a good spot, plants will spread quickly, forming a lush mat of leaves to be plucked throughout the growing season.

The leaves of wood sorrel can be plain green or marked with purple, depending on the variety.

## Quick guide

**Plant** rhizomes in fall and divisions in early spring; sow seed early spring

**Minimum** 5°F (-15°C) to maximum 86°F (30°C)

**Grow** in full or partial shade in moist, free-draining soil

**Water** before the onset of drought

**Plants grow** up to 4in (10cm) high and can spread indefinitely

**Harvest** flowers in spring and leaves in spring and summer

Step-by-step growing »

# Step-by-step growing

Try growing wood sorrel under fruit trees or in quiet, shady corners of the garden where other productive crops are unlikely to thrive. Their low carpet of leaves make ideal ground cover.

## When to grow and harvest

Propagate wood sorrel by planting rhizomes in fall, or by sowing seed, or dividing existing clumps in early spring.

| | early winter | late winter | early spring | late spring | early summer | late summer | early fall | late fall |
|---|---|---|---|---|---|---|---|---|
| sow seeds | | | • | | | | | |
| plant dormant rhizomes | | | | | | | • | • |
| plant out | | | | • | • | | | |
| harvest | | | | | • | • | • | • |
| divide plants | | | • | | | | | |

## 1 Raise from rhizomes or seeds

When the rhizomes are dormant in fall, plant them where they will grow or under cover. Fill a seed tray or modules with a combination of potting mix and leaf mold, and plant each rhizome 1in (2.5cm) deep. Water well, allow to drain, and place in a cold frame to grow on. Plants can also be raised from seed in seed trays or modules filled with the same combination of potting mix and leaf mold. Cover lightly with leaf mold, water well, and place in a cold frame. Prick out young plants once large enough to handle and pot up individually.

**The unusual** round rhizomes are roughly the size of large peas.

## 2 Plant out and aftercare

Plants should be ready to put in their final positions by late spring or early summer. Prepare the soil by digging in plenty of leaf mold. Gently tease apart young plants raised in seed trays and plant 4–6in (10–15cm) apart, in clusters rather than rows, to quickly produce a natural-looking carpet as they spread. Water in well and keep the soil moist while they establish, then only during dry spells.

**Gently tease out** the roots to help plants establish themselves in their new home.

4-6in
(10-15cm)

**Plant in** odd-numbered clusters for a natural look.

## ③ Harvest

Simply pluck the stems of individual leaves and flowers as required during the growing season, from spring into summer and sometimes fall in wet climates. Established plants will tolerate having up to one third of their leaves picked without ill effect.

**Wood sorrel** thrives in shade but can't handle too much competition, so keep the soil free from weeds.

## ④ Lift and divide clumps

To further propagate wood sorrel, large clumps can be lifted and divided in early spring as they come into growth. Ease them from the ground with a fork and gently pull sections apart. Large pieces do well planted directly in the soil, while smaller divisions are best potted up and brought on in a cold frame.

### Cook's tips

**Keep fresh**

Best eaten soon after picking, but will keep wrapped in a plastic bag in the refrigerator for 2-3 days.

**How to eat**

The fresh, lemon-and-sour-apple flavor really zings in raw leaves, but they also impart a delicate sharp taste when lightly cooked.

- Whip up a simple wood sorrel sauce by cooking leaves briefly in melted butter with cream, lemon juice, and seasoning.
- Scatter over salads to add an acidic note. This works especially well with recipes containing eggs, or in rich potato salads.
- Slice finely and combine with whipped cream to make a lovely sharp contrast to indulgent chocolate or custard desserts.
- Add to sautéed wild mushrooms just before serving.

**How to preserve**

Try freezing the leaves in ice cubes to add to drinks. Or pickle chopped leaves in a mixture of vinegar and sugar (a bit like mint sauce) and keep in the refrigerator.

## Quick guide

**Sow** during spring in a cold frame, or plant from spring to fall

**Minimum** 5°F (-15°C) to maximum 86°F (30°C)

**Grow** in moist, humus-rich soil in sun or partial shade

**Water** regularly to keep the soil constantly moist

**Plants grow** up to 1ft (30cm) tall and spread indefinitely

**Harvest** young leaves from spring to fall while plant is in growth

{  Level 1 easy }

# Fish mint

*Houttuynia cordata*

The name may not be familiar, but it's likely a form of fish mint already grows in your garden, since the multicolored cultivar 'Chameleon' is a popular ground cover plant. It is the plain green species, however, that is such a prized Asian herb, with its red-edged leaves and slightly fishy, cilantro-and-orange flavor.

## What is it?

This herbaceous perennial hails from Southeast Asia, where it grows in moist, shady places and is widely used as a herb in local cuisine, and as a treatment in traditional Chinese medicine. Western gardeners usually only value fish mint for its attractive carpets of foliage and white summer flowers. It flourishes in moist soils and pond margins, where the plant can easily become invasive thanks to long stems that grow their own roots, which enable it to spread rapidly.

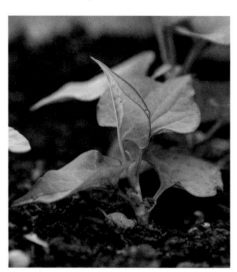

**Fish mint spreads** at a rapid pace, so if you have limited space just grow in a pot.

### When to grow and harvest

Protect spring-sown seeds in a cold frame for reliable germination, or divide existing plants in spring.

| | early winter | late winter | early spring | late spring | early summer | late summer | early fall | late fall |
|---|---|---|---|---|---|---|---|---|
| sow indoors | | | • | • | | | | |
| plant seedlings | | | | | • | • | | |
| plant pot-grown | | | • | • | • | • | • | |
| harvest | | | | | • | • | • | |

## How do I grow it?

Fish mint is hardy and easy to grow in soils that do not dry out. It is best grown in containers or planted out in a bucket with the bottom cut out and 3in (8cm) of the rim above ground, otherwise given the right conditions it can becomes invasive.

## 1 Sow seeds

For reliable germination, seed is best sown in the shelter of a cold frame or cool greenhouse. Fill a seed tray with potting mix, sow seeds thinly across the surface, and cover lightly with potting mix before watering thoroughly and allowing to drain. Keep the potting mix consistently moist. When seedlings are large enough to handle, gently prick out into 3in (7.5cm) pots and harden them off to acclimatize to outdoor conditions (see p.62).

## 2 Plant out

Plant seedlings 18in (45cm) apart and water in well. You can also plant container-raised specimens any time from spring to early fall. Water in generously and during dry weather until established. Alternatively, grow plants outdoors in large containers to restrict growth; one plant will fill a 12in (30cm) pot. Use peat-free potting mix with some loam-based mix added to help retain moisture. Water pots regularly—daily in hot summer weather.

## 3 Aftercare and harvest

In frost-prone areas, the roots can be damaged or killed during severe winters, particularly on wet soils and in pots. Protect them by adding a thick mulch of potting mix once the foliage has died back. Patchy or slow growth is most likely to be due to dry soil conditions and should be remedied by regular watering. Harvest leaves by snipping off the tips of young shoots. Stop picking if leaves become bitter during fall or are knocked back by frosts.

{ Level 1 easy }

# Water celery

*Oenanthe javanica*

With a flavor similar to celery, combined with a hint of parsley and carrot, this vigorous perennial is hardy and easy to grow in any pond margin or damp border. While water celery is completely safe to eat, others of the *Oenanthe* genus are extremely toxic, so always check the Latin name on the label before consuming.

## What is it?

Water celery is a perennial native to the river banks, lake shores, and paddy fields of eastern Asia, where it spreads by creeping stems to form large colonies. Its flat umbels of tiny white flowers are typical of the Apiaceae family, which includes cow parsley and carrots. The vitamin- and mineral-rich stems and leaves are eaten across its native range. The young shoots are an esteemed spring vegetable in Japan. It is also a popular ground cover plant for pond margins and readily available in garden centers.

**The pink variegated** cultivar 'Flamingo' provides a burst of color and is just as tasty as the standard green species.

### When to grow and harvest

Sow seeds under cover in spring for planting out in summer, or plant container-raised plants throughout the growing season.

| | early winter | late winter | early spring | late spring | early summer | late summer | early fall | late fall |
|---|---|---|---|---|---|---|---|---|
| sow indoors | | | ● | ● | | | | |
| plant seedlings | | | | | ● | ● | | |
| plant pot-grown | | | ● | ● | ● | ● | ● | |
| harvest | | | | | ● | ● | ● | ● |

## How do I grow it?

Find space for plants at the edge of a pond or in a damp border, where they will quickly form attractive clumps of foliage. Place in full sun for the best displays of the pretty white flowers. Plants tolerate drier soils if given shade and watered well.

 **1** ## Sow seeds

In spring, sow seeds on the surface of moist potting mix in a seed tray and cover lightly with potting mix. Place in a cold frame or cool greenhouse and keep damp until seeds germinate; this can take several weeks and is often erratic. When seedlings are large enough to handle, pot them into individual pots and grow on in a cold frame. In summer, harden off the seedlings (see p.62) to acclimatize them to outdoor conditions.

## 2 Plant out and aftercare

Plant seedlings 30in (75cm) apart and water in well if not in wet soil. Container-raised specimens can be planted anytime after the last frosts until fall. Water well and plant to the same depth as they grew in their pots. These tough plants look after themselves in wet conditions but need regular watering in drier locations. Remove faded stems and leaves in early winter and apply a thick mulch of potting mix (unless growing in a pond) to shield roots from frost.

## 3 Harvest and propagation

In late spring, harvest the entire young stem and leaves by cutting it at the base; stems become tough and unpalatable later in the growing season. Leaves can be picked as a herb into fall. Water celery spreads by rooting underground stems (stolons), which makes propagation easy as growth begins in late spring. Simply lift and split a section into pieces with healthy roots and shoots. Pot these up and grow on outdoors, ready for planting by late summer.

**Beneath the papery** skin, the flesh of turmeric rhizomes is deep orange and fragrant.

**Level 2**
*moderate*

# Turmeric

*Curcuma longa*

Turmeric spice comes from the rhizomes of the turmeric plant, which are dried and ground into the colorful powder. Fresh turmeric has a more powerful flavor than powder, full of citrus zest and pepperiness, and it is well worth growing plants for a ready supply of rhizomes with superfood health benefits.

## What is it?

Turmeric is a perennial plant native to Southeast Asia. From the same family as ginger, turmeric looks similar in growth but the leaves are broader, and it can reach up to 3ft (1m) in height. When added to a curry, dahl, or tagine, turmeric gives an earthy, slightly bitter flavor. Turmeric is known to contain antioxidants and to have anticarcinogenic effects–its popularity in traditional Ayurvedic medicine has long been established. The reddish-brown coloring from the dried rhizome is also used in the manufacture of cosmetics and dyes for clothing and carpets.

**Turmeric leaves** can also be used to flavor dishes and have the added benefit of not staining clothes.

In Indian weddings, turmeric is applied to the face and arms of the bride and groom as part of the traditional Haldi ceremony.

## How do I grow it?

Turmeric grows best in warm or hot climates, so keep it in a greenhouse if you live somewhere cool. Grow plants in pots of moisture-retentive potting mix in the greenhouse or as a foliage houseplant. Provide warmth, plenty of water, and a humid atmosphere, and feed during the growing season. Turmeric can be overwintered in a moderately warm greenhouse in a dormant state by drying out the potting mix. It is usually reluctant to emerge the following year, and may not appear until late spring or even early summer, but do not give up hope!

## Quick guide

**Plant** in pots in spring so they get a full growing season to become established

**Minimum** 75°F (20°C) to maximum 86°F (30°C)

**Grow** outdoors in warm climates and in a greenhouse in cooler climates

**Keep** constantly moist in the growing season; reduce watering in cooler conditions

**Plants** can reach 3ft (1m) in height and 2ft (60cm) in spread

**Harvest** the leaves and rhizomes in spring and summer

**Step-by-step growing »**

# Step-by-step growing

Turmeric is better grown in containers in cooler and temperate climates. Choose a warm and sheltered spot to encourage the best growth, and try to keep the humidity high around the plants.

### When to grow and harvest
Plant rhizomes in early spring to break dormancy. Harvest rhizomes at the very end of the growing season.

|  | early winter | late winter | early spring | late spring | early summer | late summer | early fall | late fall |
|---|---|---|---|---|---|---|---|---|
| plant rhizomes |  |  | • |  |  |  |  |  |
| transplant |  |  |  | • | • |  |  |  |
| harvest |  |  |  |  |  |  | • | • |

## 1 Sprout rhizomes

Begin by breaking the dormancy of the rhizomes. Fill 3½in (9cm) pots with soil-based growing mix combined with 20 percent multi-purpose growing mix; this mix holds moisture for longer and conducts heat well. Plant one rhizome to a pot, 2in (5cm) below the surface. Place the pots in a propagator or on heated mats, set to an ideal temperature of 86°F (30°C). Once the rhizomes have sprouted, grow in a sunny spot at 68°F (20°C).

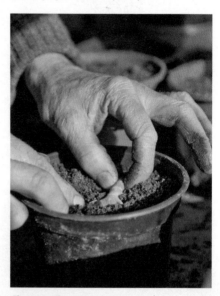

**Choose plump** and undamaged rhizomes for planting.

## 2 Grow and transplant

Keep the medium constantly moist. Transfer plants to their final growing location once growth reaches 8in (20cm). Turmeric needs to be kept at 68°F (20°C) throughout the growing season, so in cooler climates they are best grown under cover in large containers with several plants to a pot.

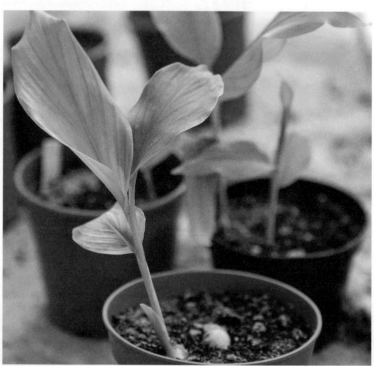

**Grow plants in the same** moisture-retentive growing mix that you used for sprouting the rhizomes.

## 3 Aftercare and harvest

Keep the growing mix moist at all times when in growth. Feed every two weeks with a liquid general fertilizer and provide an occasional boost of liquid seaweed.

If growing in containers under cover, regularly mist plants with lukewarm water to stop the leaf margins from yellowing and to discourage red spider mite, which turns the leaves mottled and yellow, weaves fine webs, and thrives in dry air.

Once established, pick leaves only occasionally and not from the same plant. To harvest the rhizomes, wait for the leaves to yellow and start to die back before digging them up.

**Container-grown** plants can be moved outdoors when temperatures hit 68°F (20°C), but keep misting.

## 4 Winter care

Plants still in leaf can be overwintered in a warm greenhouse or brought indoors and grown as a houseplant. Maintain humidity by keeping them in the bathroom, or set on trays of pebbles filled with water to the bottom of the pot. Mist occasionally. Transplant to pots one size larger in spring once they outgrow their current pots. Rhizomes for sprouting next year can be overwintered in a dormant state in pots of dry growing mix at 54–59°F (12–15°C), watering occasionally to keep them from drying out completely.

---

### Cook's tips

#### Keep fresh
Use the leaves at once. Wrap rhizomes in a paper towel and store in the fridge.

#### How to eat
Prepare the rhizomes by peeling and then grating them or finely chopping. Use fresh turmeric in Indian or Middle Eastern recipes by either processing it into a paste, or adding to browned onions with garlic and dried spices and frying for a couple of minutes.

- Squeeze the juice from grated turmeric and add to coffee with warm milk and honey for a turmeric latte.
- Add whole to a smoothie mix before processing.
- The flavor of fresh turmeric works very well in egg-based dishes, such as omelettes.
- Wrap the leaves around Asian dumplings before steaming, or use as a pouch for baking whole fish or fillets.

#### How to preserve
Place clean and dry rhizomes in a plastic bag with as little air as possible and freeze. Turmeric pieces can also be pickled.

{ **Level 2**
moderate }

# Wasabi

*Wasabia japonica*

The roots of the wasabi plant taste a lot like horseradish and, because it is comparatively slow-growing—hence expensive to produce—most wasabi paste outside of Japan is a fake concoction of horseradish and mustard. Grow your own to avoid imitations!

## What is it?

Native to Japan, wasabi is found in soggy ground by misty mountain rivers. A slow-growing, hardy perennial, it has glossy, heart-shaped leaves and spikes of small white flowers in late spring. A well-grown plant can also be a garden feature, and thrives in cool, cloudy summers. The Japanese prize *sawa* (water-grown) wasabi is of higher quality than *oka* (field-grown). Commercial paste is made by grinding dried roots into powder, but finely grated fresh roots provide an even stronger and cleaner taste. Leaves, stalks, flowers, and roots are used to make the pickle *wasabi-zuke*.

> *Wasabi has been so revered in Japan that throughout its history retired shōguns, or emperors, were given plantations to tend in retirement.*

**Young wasabi leaves** can also be eaten and have a mild taste, which is more gentle on the tongue than the roots.

## How do I grow it?

If you lack streams of fresh, flowing water in your garden, just grow wasabi in moist soil in the shade. Roots grow best in areas where conditions are cool in fall and spring. Plants will also flourish in a large pot of loam-based mix, fed in spring with slow-release general fertilizer and kept constantly moist. Young roots have the best flavor, so divide up healthy plants every 2 years in early spring, and grow on in an unheated greenhouse or cold frame, before planting out in late spring the following year. Alternatively, propagate by detaching offsets from well-established plants in spring and replant.

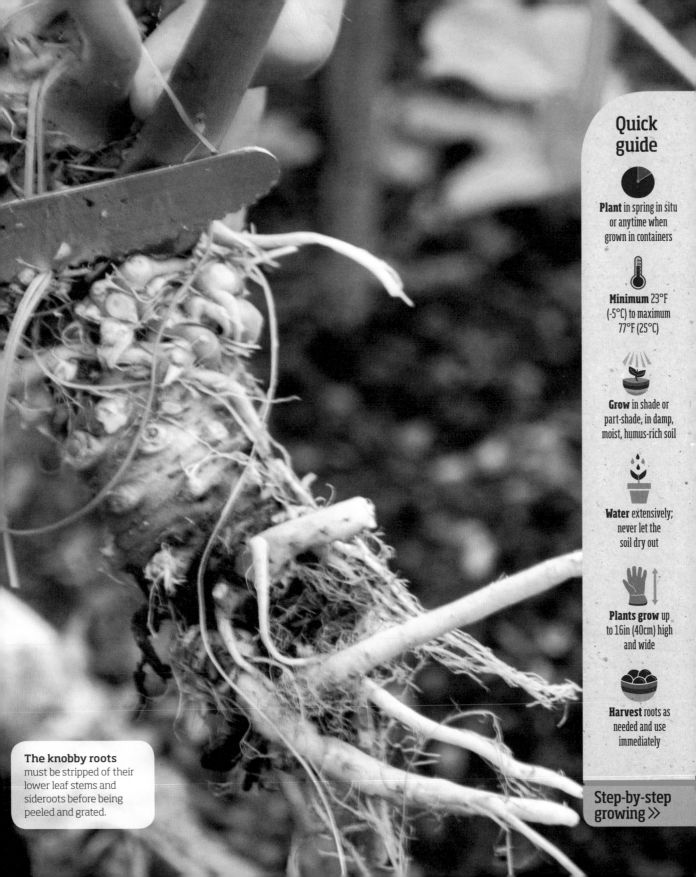

**The knobby roots** must be stripped of their lower leaf stems and sideroots before being peeled and grated.

## Quick guide

**Plant** in spring in situ or anytime when grown in containers

**Minimum** 23°F (-5°C) to maximum 77°F (25°C)

**Grow** in shade or part-shade, in damp, moist, humus-rich soil

**Water** extensively; never let the soil dry out

**Plants grow** up to 16in (40cm) high and wide

**Harvest** roots as needed and use immediately

Step-by-step growing »

# Step-by-step growing

Buy container-raised plants to start growing wasabi; afterward, you can maintain your collection with offsets and plantlets from harvested roots. Protect from damage by slugs and cabbage caterpillars.

**When to grow and harvest**
Plant out after the last frosts. Harvest leaves and flowers as they appear and rhizomes as needed.

| | early winter | late winter | early spring | late spring | early summer | late summer | early fall | late fall |
|---|---|---|---|---|---|---|---|---|
| plant | | | | | ● | ● | | |
| harvest | ● | ● | ● | ● | ● | ● | ● | ● |

## ① Grow on and prep the soil

Transplant container-raised plants into 3½in (9cm) pots of loam-based mix and grow on in a shady spot, potting up as they grow, until the danger of frost has passed. Wasabi grows best when its feet are in clean, nutrient-rich, running water. It will grow in a damp, shady position in the garden or at the edge of a pond, although the roots will rot if the soil is too wet. Improve the drainage, structure, and nutrient levels of the soil ahead of planting by digging in plenty of well-rotted organic matter; leave the soil to settle.

**Mail-order plants** often arrive wrapped in damp burlap. Transplant them immediately into individual pots.

## ② Plant out

Water the plants in their containers and allow them to drain. Dig a hole in the ground slightly larger than the pot, ease the plant from the pot, and gently tease out the roots. Water the bottom of the hole if the soil is dry. Once the water has drained away, plant the wasabi so the potting mix surface is just above the level of the surrounding soil. Firm in the soil and water thoroughly. If growing in containers, plant in loam-based mix combined with a few handfuls of grit to improve drainage.

**Give plants a good soak** before planting out to keep them growing well until the roots get established.

## ③ Aftercare

Feed in spring with slow-release general fertilizer and keep plants well-watered. A mulch of potting medium or gravel will help lock in moisture. Gravel also works as a deterrent to slugs and snails, and there are numerous other environmentally friendly ways to combat them: encourage predators like ground beetles, frogs, toads, and thrushes; use nematodes; place copper tape around pots; or douse plants with garlic spray. Cabbage caterpillars also find the leaves tasty, as the plant is in the Brassica family. Protect with horticultural fleece or fine mesh netting placed over a frame of stakes; this allows a gap between the net and leaves, so the adult insects cannot reach them to lay eggs.

**If temperatures get too high** in summer, plants may die back, but once the weather cools they will produce another flush of leaves.

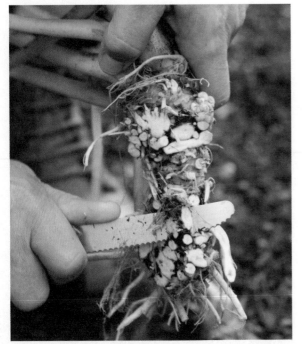

## ④ Winter care and harvest

Remove and compost the leaves when they die back in fall, and protect from cold weather over winter by covering with horticultural fleece or a layer of bracken or straw. It takes about 24 months for the rhizomes to reach harvestable size. Carefully dig up the plant, harvest the main root and leaves, then tease the small offsets or plantlets apart and replant. The whole plant is edible, so eat the leaf stems, leaves, and flowers, too.

**Wasabi roots** need 2 years or more for the flavor to mature.

### Cook's tips

**Keep fresh**

Store roots in the refrigerator, wrapped in moistened paper towel. Rinse with cold water every few days and they will last up to 1 month.

**How to eat**

Young leaves can be eaten raw or sautéed. Grate the roots for pastes and as a flavoring. Roots reach maximum heat 5 minutes after grating; the heat starts to decline after 20 minutes.

- Add the paste to a hollandaise sauce and serve with poached, grilled, or roasted salmon. The sauce also goes well with pan-fried steak.
- Grate to add flavor to soups and noodles, in sashimi and sushi, and on seafood.
- Wasabi paste gives a special twist to deviled eggs.
- Mix grated root with soy sauce and sesame oil in a marinade for chicken.
- Use the leaves and flowers as an alternative to watercress or arugula in salads.

**How to preserve**

Wasabi root lasts up to 1 year if made into a paste and kept in the refrigerator. Try pickling the leaves and flowers.

{ Level 2 moderate }

# Japanese ginger

*Zingiber mioga*

If you are a fan of ginger and would like to grow your own but don't live in a tropical climate, try cultivating this closely related, cold-tolerant species. Unlike conventional root ginger, it is the stems and peculiar flower buds of this variety that are harvested.

## What is it?

Exotic in appearance yet extremely hardy, *Zingiber mioga* is a tall, herbaceous perennial plant found in the wild in parts of China, northern Vietnam, South Korea, and Japan, where it grows on shady slopes and mountain valleys among mixed and deciduous woodlands. The short-lived, orchidlike flowers appear in midsummer at soil level or just peeping out from the soil. The plant is deeply rooted in Japanese culture, where annual *myoga matsuri* festivals are held to celebrate the mythology and folklore associated with the plant.

*Of the more than 20,000 ancient family crests in Japan, one of the top 10 most common heraldic devices depicts two myoga flower buds facing each other.*

**The species has** fresh green leaves, and there are variegated cultivars available.

## How do I grow it?

Plants are grown from rhizomes (underground stems similar to roots and tubers) planted in spring. You should only need to buy rhizomes once, as these perennial plants will sprout again each spring after dying back in fall, and you can refresh and expand your stock by dividing established plants or propagating from sections of new rhizomes. As a woodland plant, *Zingiber mioga* will thrive in part-shade and prefers a humus-rich, moisture-retentive, yet well-draining soil. Plants grow well in large containers, and the attractive foliage and fascinating flowers make it an appealing plant for balconies and small courtyard gardens. Although it is the hardiest member of the ginger family, plants benefit from a thick mulch in fall as protection against winter chills.

The pinkish flower **buds** are known as *myoga no ko* or "children of myoga" in Japan and are used as a spicy garnish.

## Quick guide

**Plant in spring** once the danger of frost has passed

**Minimum** -9°F (-23°C) to maximum 82°F (28°C)

**Grow in** sun or part-shade in organic-rich soil

**Water** frequently to keep plants and soil constantly moist, but avoid waterlogging

**Plants grow** up to 3ft (1m) in height and spread to 5ft (1.5m)

**Harvest** shoots in spring and flower buds in summer

Step-by-step growing »

# Step-by-step growing

Japanese ginger can be grown from rhizomes or container-raised plants available from specialty nurseries. They will thrive in a rich, free-draining, slightly acidic soil that doesn't get waterlogged in winter.

### When to grow and harvest
This ginger can be planted outdoors from late winter. Harvest new shoots in spring and flower buds in summer.

|  | early winter | late winter | early spring | late spring | early summer | late summer | early fall | late fall |
|---|---|---|---|---|---|---|---|---|
| plant |  | • | • |  |  |  |  |  |
| harvest |  |  | • | • |  | • |  |  |

## ① Plant out

Dig in plenty of organic matter and leave the soil to settle before planting. Plant container-raised plants so that the soil is at the same level as the potting mix. In heavier soils prone to waterlogging, add a ¾in (2cm) layer of gravel at the base of the planting hole as a precaution. Plant rhizomes with a 1¼in (3cm) layer of soil above them. Space plants 12-16in (30-40cm) apart. Japanese ginger is a vigorous grower and, once established, just a few plants will provide a plentiful harvest, so there should be no need to plant multiple rows.

**Plant the bare-rooted rhizomes** so that the tapered ends, from which new shoots emerge, are pointing upward.

## ② Growing in containers

Japanese ginger also does well in pots. Grow in free-draining, bark-based potting medium with 20 percent chopped bark, and feed a general liquid fertilizer every 2 weeks.

**If temperatures are set to drop** below 14°F (-10°C), move container-grown plants to a sheltered spot or under cover.

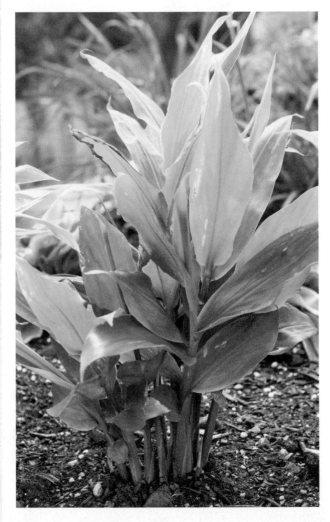

**Japanese ginger** is a
woodland plant and likes to
grow in soil enriched with
leaf mold and bark.

### 3 Aftercare

Keep plants constantly moist,
but never waterlogged.
Protect young plants and
new spring growth from
slugs and snails using any
number of environmentally
friendly methods, such as
organic traps, nematodes,
garlic spray, and copper tape
around containers.

Unless plants are growing
in a woodland border where
there is natural leaf fall,
Japanese ginger benefits
greatly from a thick mulch of
leaf mold applied in spring
and fall, and also for winter
protection.

Propagate in spring by
dividing established clumps
as they start into growth or
replanting 6-8in (15-20cm)
sections of rhizome taken
from robust plants.

### 4 Harvest

Wait until plants have had a year to establish themselves
before harvesting. Cut a few young shoots from each
plant when less than 16in (40cm) long. Look out for
flowers from midsummer. Pick when they are still tight
buds, but leave a few for their spectacular blooms.

**Flowers form** at the plant
base and emerge out of the soil.

## Cook's tips

### Keep fresh
Stems and flower buds keep
for 10 days in the refrigerator,
wrapped in paper towel.

### How to eat
Chopped flower buds and
shoots are used raw as a
garnish for many Asian
dishes, especially sashimi
and sushi. They can also be
cooked whole or sliced, and
added as a flavoring for
stir-fries and stews.

- Scatter sliced shoots and
  chopped buds over miso soup
  and soba noodles.
- Skewer buds between cubes
  of marinated meat or tofu and
  cook on the grill.
- Chop the buds in half and fry
  in tempura batter; great with
  seafood tempura.
- The flavor goes particularly
  well with eggplant: try
  sprinkling over chunks roasted
  with soy and honey.
- Try using the shoots in place
  of lemongrass.

### How to preserve
Make a quick pickle by boiling
the buds for 1 minute in rice
or cider vinegar mixed with
sugar. Keeps for up to 1
week in the refrigerator.

# Tea

*Camellia sinensis*

**Level 2** *moderate*

## Quick guide

**Plant** in spring when the final frost has passed

**Minimum** 32°F (0°C) to maximum 84°F (29°C)

**Grow** in moist, acidic, free-draining soil, or citrus and palm mix

**Water** regularly with rainwater to keep medium moist

**Plants can grow** up to 20ft (6m) tall, so keep well pruned

**Pick** young leaves and buds in spring, and flowers in fall

Most of the world's tea is made in China and India, and you might imagine the leaves come from some exotic plant. However, the tea plant is in fact a species of camellia, a type of evergreen shrub grown in the West for its beautiful flowers for at least 200 years.

## What is it?

*Camellia sinensis* is a long-lived shrub native to East Asia, where it is found growing in the wild in acidic soil in woodlands. The young leaves and leaf buds of commercially grown shrubs are harvested and processed to make tea. There are "small leaf" and "large leaf" varieties; the latter not only have larger leaves and flowers, but the leaves are more widely spaced and have greater vigor. The flowers burst into bloom in late summer and fall and can also be added to the teapot.

**The dainty white flowers** produce a mass of prominent golden stamens and look especially attractive against the foil of glossy foliage.

### When to grow and harvest

Plant in late fall, late winter, or early spring. Harvest leaf tips in spring and flowers in fall.

| | early winter | late winter | early spring | late spring | early summer | late summer | early fall | late fall |
|---|---|---|---|---|---|---|---|---|
| plant | | ● | ● | | | | | ● |
| harvest | | | ● | ● | | | ● | ● |

## How do I grow it?

Grow from container-raised shrubs planted out in acidic soil in a partly shaded, sheltered location. Protect from frost, cold winds, and sun scorch. For the first few winters, cover young plants with horticultural fleece, or move potted plants to a cool greenhouse or conservatory with good air circulation. Water with rainwater, which is slightly acidic; use tap water only in emergencies.

### 1 Plant out

If planting a number of specimens, leave 35in (90cm) between each plant. Water plants with rainwater and allow to drain before planting. If the soil is dry, water the bottom of the hole and scatter root-boosting mycorrhizal fungi around the base. Plant so the potting mix surface is level with the surrounding soil. In alkaline areas, grow in containers of citrus and palm mix with 20 percent small-grade chipped bark added for drainage.

## ② Aftercare and pruning

Mulch in spring with an acidic pine needle mulch, and feed citrus and palm fertilizer at the same time. Water until established, and then in drought. After the frosts, while the plant is dormant, cut back last year's growth by one third or a half to just above a leaf. The new shoots will produce more sideshoots and leaves. Do this annually to create a compact, productive bush. To enjoy the flowers, prune as above for the first 3 years, then allow to grow naturally.

## ③ Harvest

Do not overpick in the early years; just take a few leaves from each shrub until they are established and growing strongly. After that, pick all you like. Traditionally, the uppermost pair of leaves and leaf bud at the tip of each stem are picked. Older leaves can also be used to make tea, but the flavor is bitter and quite different to the young, tender shoots. Pick the flowers when they have opened fully but aren't yet going over.

## Quick guide

**Sow** under cover in spring, then plant out in warmer weather or grow on under cover

**Minimum** 50°F (10°C) to maximum 86°F (30°C)

**Grow on** a sunny, sheltered site in free-draining soil

**Keep moist** but avoid waterlogging

**Plants grow** up to 24in (60cm) in both height and spread

**Harvest** leaves after flowering, once plants are well established

**Level 2** *moderate*

# Sweetleaf
### *Stevia rebaudiana*

The leaves of *Stevia rebaudiana* are many times sweeter than sugar, yet calorie-free, and are used commercially as a sugar substitute. Grow your own plants at home and you can use the fresh leaves to enjoy a sweet hit without the guilt.

## What is it?

This tender perennial of the daisy family, with attractive foliage and tiny white flowers, is native to Brazil and Paraguay, where the leaves are traditionally used as a treatment for colic, stomach problems, and even as a contraceptive. In commercial processing, the leaves are steeped in water, filtered, purified, and dried to produce crystallized stevia extract. But home gardeners can simply harvest the leaves after flowering and use fresh or dried.

### When to grow and harvest

Sow in spring, transplanting outdoors or growing on indoors. Harvest leaves after plants have flowered.

| | early winter | late winter | early spring | late spring | early summer | late summer | early fall | late fall |
|---|---|---|---|---|---|---|---|---|
| sow indoors | | • | • | | | | | |
| plant out | | | | • | • | | | |
| harvest | | | | | • | • | • | |

**Grow sweetleaf outdoors** as a perennial where temperatures remain above 50°F (10°C), or as an annual plant in cooler climates.

## How do I grow it?

Sow from seed or buy plants from a specialty nursery. Although not hardy, sweetleaf can be grown in cooler climates as an indoor or greenhouse perennial, or an annual in borders or containers. Grow in a sunny position in free-draining soil, but keep it moist. Feed to encourage healthy growth and pinch back sideshoots so the plant becomes a bush rather than a leafy stick.

## 1 Sow indoors

In spring, sow indoors in trays or modules onto the surface of moist seed-starting mix, and cover with a fine layer of potting mix or vermiculite. Leave in a warm place in a plastic bag or put in a propagator at 77–81°F (25–27°C) to maintain humidity; seeds take 1 or 2 weeks to germinate. When seedlings are large enough to handle, prick them out into pots of all-purpose mix.

## 2 Grow on or plant out

Transplant into larger pots before plants become pot-bound, and either continue to grow under cover as a container plant or in a greenhouse border, or plant outdoors where soil temperatures are at least 50°F (10°C), after first hardening off (see p.62). Choose a site in rich, moist, well-draining soil in full sun. Space rows 20-24in (50-60cm) apart, with 18in (45cm) between plants. Perennial plants often keep their leaves, but some may fall due to low light.

## 3 Aftercare and harvest

Pinch back the growing tips to encourage branching and to increase leaf production. Feed a general fertilizer every 2 weeks when in growth, and water when the potting mix surface is dry. Control slugs with environmentally friendly pellets and traps, or biological controls, and encourage natural predators. Cut back to 1in (2.5cm) in spring to encourage growth. Once established, harvest a proportion of leaves from each plant as required.

**Plant in spring** to allow a full growing season for plants to establish

**Minimum** -4°F (-20°C) to maximum 77°F (25°C)

**Grow** in sun or part-shade in damp or soggy conditions

**Keep** well-watered, especially if growing in containers

**Reaches** 4ft (1.2m) high with a spread of 2ft (60cm)

**Harvest leaves** before flowers appear, and pick flowers before they start to fade

{ Level 1 easy }

# Meadowsweet

*Filipendula ulmaria*

A hardy, moisture-loving plant, meadowsweet bears a succession of edible, frothy, white plumes from late spring to the first frosts. The flowers have a strong flavor, perhaps best described as marzipan with a metallic tang, while the leaves contain an aspirinlike compound and are often used in pain-relieving herbal remedies.

## What is it?

Meadowsweet is a compact, clump-forming, herbaceous perennial whose leaves and stems die back in winter, with new shoots appearing in the spring. It is found in damp and soggy soils, near water courses and wet woodlands, throughout Europe and West Asia. The buds, blossoms, seeds, and leaves are all edible. The flowers were once used to flavor mead, while the smell of the leaves is similar to cucumber.

### When to grow and harvest

Plant out container-raised plants in early spring and the blooms should be ready for picking by early summer.

|  | early winter | late winter | early spring | late spring | early summer | late summer | early fall | late fall |
|---|---|---|---|---|---|---|---|---|
| plant |  |  | • | • | • |  |  |  |
| harvest |  |  |  |  | • | • | • |  |

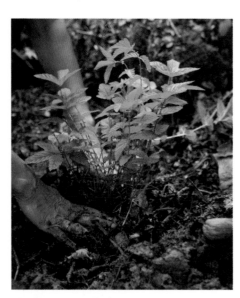

**Meadowsweet thrives** in wet soil. If growing in a container, use a loam-based mix.

## How do I grow it?

Meadowsweet is best grown from young plants bought from a garden center or nursery in spring. All it needs for a happy life is wet ground and sunshine. The cultivars 'Aurea', with bright yellow leaves in spring fading to light green by midsummer, and 'Variegata', whose leaves have yellow splashes and margins, make fine feature plants for containers.

### 1 Plant out

Improve the soil by digging in well-rotted organic matter. Water the plant in its container and allow to drain. Dig a hole slightly larger than the container, water the bottom of the hole, and then scatter over a root-booster of mycorrhizal fungi when the water drains off. Remove the plant from its pot and gently tease out the roots. Position it in the hole and backfill with potting mix until level with the soil surface. Water in thoroughly.

## ② Aftercare

To avoid the soil drying out, mulch around the plant with a 1¼in (3cm) layer of well-rotted organic matter in spring, and water constantly during the growing season. Place container-grown plants in part shade to avoid leaf scorch and so that the growing medium dries out slowly. If soil conditions are too dry, the leaves will shrivel and suffer from powdery mildew, a whitish fungus that appears on the leaf surfaces. Feed a slow-release general fertilizer in spring.

## ③ Harvest and winter care

Pick flower heads when most of the flowers have opened and before they start to fade. Pick leaves young and fresh, but not too many from one plant. Cut back plants in fall and keep weed free through the winter. Move container plants into a sheltered position under a tree, at the base of a sheltered wall, or into a garage or shed, to protect from frost. Just before growth starts again in spring, transplant into a pot one size larger.

# FRUIT

# Kiwiberry

*Actinidia arguta*

**Level 3** advanced

The size of a large grape, kiwiberries are the diminutive cousins of the fuzzy brown kiwi fruit common to supermarkets. No need to peel–these sweet, moreish berries can be enjoyed plucked straight off the rapidly growing vines.

## What is it?

The kiwiberry is a vigorous, hardy, perennial climbing plant native to more northerly parts of East Asia. Most varieties have male and female flowers on different plants, which means at least one plant of each sex is needed to produce fruit. Male plants must be growing around 24in (60cm) from females to pollinate successfully, though a single male can pollinate several females. The job of transferring pollen can be left to insects, or you can pollinate by hand with a paintbrush.

### When to grow and harvest

Plants produce fruit 3–4 years after planting. Prune regularly, and harvest throughout summer and fall.

| | early winter | late winter | early spring | late spring | early summer | late summer | early fall | late fall |
|---|---|---|---|---|---|---|---|---|
| plant | | | | ● | | | | |
| harvest | | | | | ● | ● | ● | ● |

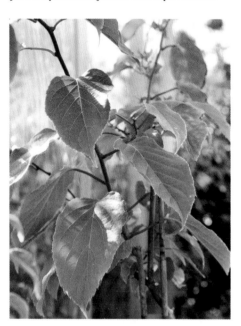

**The kiwiberry vine** has attractively colored red stems and large, heart-shaped leaves.

## How do I grow it?

Kiwiberries can be grown without shelter in warm climates. In cooler areas young shoots can be damaged by frost in spring, so protect with horticultural fleece or old net curtains. Fruits need a long growing season to ripen and develop best against a sunny wall or pergola, with the stems supported by sturdy, free-standing galvanized wires set 12in (30cm) apart.

## ❶ Planting and care

Buy container-raised plants in spring and plant outdoors about 12in (30cm) from the base of a wall or pergola and 10–15ft (3–4.5m) apart. Water thoroughly after planting and mulch with well-rotted organic matter. In late winter, mulch around the base of the plant with well-rotted manure. Apply slow-release, general-purpose fertilizer around the base in spring, as growth starts. Keep moist during the growing season.

## ② Initial training

After planting, cut back the main stem to 12in (30cm). Tie the new leading shoot to a cane attached vertically to horizontal wires. Tie in a pair of parallel sideshoots along each wire to form the main arms of the vine. Let laterals (sideshoots from main stems) grow out from these arms at roughly 20in (50cm) intervals and pinch back the tips when they produce 5 leaves. If growing up a pergola, allow one main stem to reach the top, then fan out sideshoots.

## ③ Aftercare and harvest

The following winter, cut existing laterals back to 3 or 4 buds beyond the last fruited stems. Thereafter, cut back each year about one quarter to one third of the oldest lateral stems to a single bud. Vines also need summer pruning to keep under control: pinch back any sideshoots growing from the laterals and main arms. Once the fruit has formed, pinch back the laterals, leaving 4 or 5 leaves beyond the maturing fruit. Harvest when fruits soften slightly but are still firm.

## Quick guide

**Plant** in spring so plants have a whole growing season to establish

**Minimum** 45°F (7°C) to maximum 95°F (35°C)

**Plant in** specialty citrus potting mix and allow plenty of light

**Keep moist** but not waterlogged; reduce watering in winter

**Plants** in containers can reach up to 5ft (1.5m) in height

**Fruits** can be harvested all year round

## Finger lime
### Level 3 advanced
*Citrus australasica*

The finger lime is a remarkable plant. Open up its fingerlike fruit, and tiny pearls with the taste of lime and grapefruit burst out under the pressure. Widely used to garnish seafood, the pearls have the exquisite texture of caviar and "pop" in the mouth.

### What is it?

As its Latin name *Citrus australasica* suggests, the finger lime is a native of Australia, where it thrives as a thorny understory plant in the rainforests of Queensland and New South Wales. Fruits can grow up to 4¾in (12cm) long and usually have green-yellow skin and pulp, but there is a naturally occurring red-fleshed form, *Citrus australasica* var. *sanguinea*, and lots of colorful cultivars, too. When ripe, the fruits feel plump and detach easily from the plant—there will be plenty of picking to do!

### When to grow and harvest

Finger lime is in active growth in spring and summer, but can produce fruits throughout the year.

| | early winter | late winter | early spring | late spring | early summer | late summer | early fall | late fall |
|---|---|---|---|---|---|---|---|---|
| plant | | | | • | • | | | |
| move outdoors | | | | | • | | | |
| move indoors | | | | | | | • | |
| harvest | • | • | • | • | • | • | • | • |

### How do I grow it?

In cool climates, finger limes are best grown in containers so they can be moved outdoors when it's warm enough and brought back in under cover when it's not. Find them a warm, sheltered, sunny position in summer and bring indoors well before the first frosts. Overwinter plants in a moderately warm, bright, draught-free place. Repot in spring before they become pot-bound.

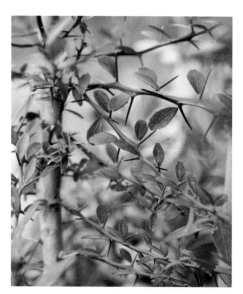

**In spring, pinch off** the ends of young shoots with your finger and thumb to encourage branching, but watch out for the thorns.

## 1 Plant and move outdoors

From late spring, plant container-raised plants in pots of well-drained, gritty, acidic potting mix, such as a citrus potting mix. Move plants outdoors after the last frosts, placing them first in shade and then moving them into the sun over several days to avoid scorching the leaves. Plants stop growing above 95°F (35°C), indoors and outdoors, so ventilate as required.

## ② Summer care

In summer, water from above with lukewarm water, soaking the potting mix but not leaving it waterlogged; tap water is fine if it's not artificially softened. Feed summer citrus feed weekly and spray with soft soap against red spider mite and mealy bug. Move indoors before the first frosts into a spot with constant temperatures, away from dry air and with maximum light, ideally at 50°F (10°C) or more. Mist plants growing indoors regularly to maintain humidity.

## ③ Winter care and harvest

When watering in winter, err on the dry side; overwatering in winter is a common cause of death. Feed a winter citrus feed according to the manufacturer's instructions. In early spring, repot when needed into a pot one size larger. In the years they are not repotted, remove the top 2in (5cm) of old potting mix in late spring and replace with fresh potting mix. Leave fruit hanging on the tree until needed. Fruit is ripe if it feels full enough to burst and comes off the plant easily.

**The deep red berries** ripen into fall and are used to make a traditional liqueur in southern Chile.

# Chilean guava

*Ugni molinae*

**Level 2** *moderate*

This pretty, compact shrub makes an attractive, ornamental, and edible plant that is suitable for the small garden. The aromatic fruits are the size of blackcurrants, but taste like wild strawberries and bubblegum. It really should be more widely grown.

## What is it?

This hardy evergreen shrub was introduced to European and North American gardeners by the plant hunter William Lobb in 1844, who found it growing in Chile, both wild in woodlands and scrubs, and in private gardens as a fruit bush for desserts. It was hoped the shrubs would become equally popular in the northern hemisphere. Trials were undertaken and prizes offered in competitions at horticultural shows, but the plant never caught on. Perhaps its moment of glory is now!

*Chilean guava was said to have been Queen Victoria's favorite fruit because the berries have little crowns.*

**The light pink flowers** are sweetly scented and blossom from late spring.

## How do I grow it?

Chilean guava needs shelter, sunshine, and moisture to flourish, but given all that, it then requires little in the way of aftercare. The shrubs are suitable for hedging, even in small gardens, and specimens grow well in containers where their attractive, fragrant flowers can be closely appreciated. Plants need shelter from cold winds, which can scorch the leaves, and this will also help insect pollinators do their job. Unlike blueberries, Chilean guava thrives in both acidic and alkaline conditions, provided it is not shallow chalk.

## Quick guide

**Plant in spring** so it has the whole growing season to establish

**Minimum** 14°F (-10°C) to maximum 77°F (25°C)

**Grow** under shelter in full sun or part-shade, and acidic or alkaline, well-drained soil

**Water** often to keep the soil moist

**Plants grow** up to 10ft (3m) in height and spread

**Pick** the red fruits in late summer and early fall

**Step-by-step growing »**

# Step-by-step growing

Grow in a sunny site, planted out or in pots, and keep the soil or potting mix moist throughout the growing season. Provide winter protection in colder areas and exposed sites.

## When to grow and harvest
Plant in spring or early summer and enjoy the berries from late summer to early fall.

| | early winter | late winter | early spring | late spring | early summer | late summer | early fall | late fall |
|---|---|---|---|---|---|---|---|---|
| plant | | | • | • | • | | | |
| harvest | | | | | | • | • | |

## 1 Plant out

Buy container-raised plants for planting out after the last frosts. Choose a position that will shelter the evergreen leaves from cold, drying winds, otherwise it will tolerate most well-drained soil types. Mature shrubs can reach an eventual spread of 3ft (1m), so keep this in mind for spacings if planting more than one. Water the plant in its container and allow to drain. Dig a hole in the ground slightly larger than the pot, ease the plant from the pot, and gently tease out the roots. Water the bottom of the hole if the soil is dry and, once the water has drained away, scatter root-boosting mycorrhizal fungi around the base of the hole where they will come into contact with the roots. Plant the shrub so the potting mix surface is at the level of the surrounding soil and firm in. Water thoroughly and mulch with well-rotted organic matter or forest bark.

Chilean guava also grows very well in a large container. For a growing medium, use potting mix, mixed with 20 percent well-rotted organic matter or general potting medium. Place the containers in a sunny, sheltered position where you, and the insects, can enjoy the intoxicating scent of the flowers.

**If growing in a pot**, plant a single specimen in a container 14in (35cm) in diameter with a volume of 5 gallons, and pot up to a larger size as required.

14in (35cm)

**Give the container-raised shrubs** a thorough soak in their pots before planting out, so that they keep growing strongly while the roots are getting established.

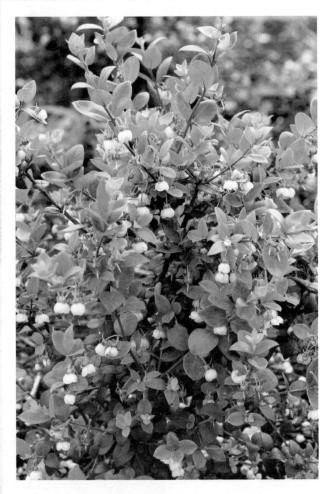

## ③ Aftercare and pruning

Mulch in spring when the soil is damp to conserve moisture and suppress weeds. If growing in pots, keep plants moist and feed in spring with slow-release general fertilizer. Repot into larger containers in late winter or early spring if they start to look pot-bound. If their site is affected by cold winds, protect over winter with horticultural fleece.

Prune in spring after the frosts. Remove dead, dying, or crossing branches and any that are badly placed, weak, or damaged. Give container plants a more general trim to keep them manageable.

**The bell-like flowers** have an understated appearance but a strong fragrance.

## ④ Harvest

Pick the cranberry-sized berries from late summer when they have taken on a deep red color. Harvest on a dry day and try a few first to check for ripeness. You may need to pick over the plant several times to gather the whole crop.

**Ripe berries** are slightly soft to the touch.

*Cook's tips*

### Keep fresh
Store dry, undamaged berries in a sealed plastic bag, or a container lined with paper towel, in the refrigerator for up to 1 week.

### How to eat
The fruits can be used in place of cranberries and blueberries in most recipes.

- Add to any fruit salad or layer in a Rumtopf.
- Make a compote by simmering the berries with a little water and sugar until they start to release their juices.
- Turn into a Chilean guava pie for pudding.
- Use in your favorite muffin or cupcake recipe instead of other fresh berries.
- Stir into the mix of a lemon polenta cake or add a layer to the base of a cake tin for an upside-down treat.
- Replaces cranberries in a sauce for roast lamb or turkey.

### How to preserve
Cook with quince and reduce down to make the traditional Chilean preserve known as *murta con membrillo*. The fruits also make excellent jams and jellies.

## Quick guide

**Plant** container-raised shrubs in spring

**Minimum** -40°F (-40°C) to maximum 86°F (30°C)

**Grow** in full sun, ideally in soil rich in organic matter and free draining

**Water frequently** to keep the soil moist

**Plants grow** up to 4ft (1.2m) in height and spread

**Harvest** ripe fruits from late spring to early summer

{ Level 1 easy }

# Honeyberry
### Lonicera caerulea varieties

This easy-to-grow shrub in the honeysuckle family produces unusually shaped, frosted-blue berries that taste like blueberries, blackberries, and raspberries rolled into one. The fruits contain high levels of vitamin C and potassium, and their antioxidant content is reported to be three times higher than that of blueberries.

## What is it?

Honeyberry is an extremely hardy shrub that grows well in most soils. Two or more plants of different varieties are needed to produce a good crop. Cultivars of *Lonicera caerulea* var. *edulis* offer some of the best eating varieties: 'Atut' is a good pollinator for 'Duet.' Another superior eating variety is *Lonicera caerulea* var. *kamtschatica*, which includes cultivars 'Larisa' and 'Rebecca' for heavy cropping and sweet flavor, and 'Maries' for a very compact habit, suitable for small gardens and containers.

### When to grow and harvest

Plant shrubs in spring and expect your first harvest up to 2 years later in late spring and early summer.

|  | early winter | late winter | early spring | late spring | early summer | late summer | early fall | late fall |
|---|---|---|---|---|---|---|---|---|
| plant |  |  | ● | ● |  |  |  |  |
| harvest |  |  |  | ● | ● |  |  |  |

**Honeyberry plants** grow attractive, sea-green foliage, and small, pale yellow flowers that appear from very late winter to early spring.

## How do I grow it?

Best grown from container-raised plants, honeyberry thrives in both acid and alkaline soils, making it a useful alternative to blueberry in nonacid soil. Its compact size and ability to grow in pots make it ideal for a small garden.

## 1 Planting and aftercare

Plant in spring after the last frost in free-draining soil enriched with garden potting mix or well-rotted manure. Water well after planting, and mulch with well-rotted organic matter or forest bark. Keep the soil moist and apply a balanced fertilizer every spring. Net the plants or grow in a fruit cage to protect berries from birds. Plants can also be grown in pots of loam-based mix and potted on into larger containers each year.

## Cook's tips

### Keep fresh
Store berries in the fridge in a sealed container lined with paper towels.

### How to eat
Eat raw or use in cooking instead of blueberries.

- Make a sauce for roast pork, venison, or duck.
- Chop into a fruity salsa for veggie burgers, with onion, chilies, cilantro, and lime juice.
- Simmer with a little water to make a compote for pancakes.

### How to preserve
Berries can be frozen or turned into jam, or try pickling in a sweetened vinegar flavored with rosemary sprigs.

## ② Pollination and harvest

Plants growing in a warm, sunny site, sheltered from the wind, tend to be good croppers, as insect pollinators are more likely to be active early in the season, when the shrubs are in flower. You can also pollinate by hand using a soft brush to transfer pollen from the flowers of one variety to another. Harvest fruits when the ripe berries have turned blue with a whitish bloom and the flesh is dark purple.

## ③ Pruning

Plants can take up to 2 years to begin fruiting. Once they've started bearing berries, give shrubs a light annual pruning from early to midsummer, after fruiting. Remove dead, diseased, dying, crossing, and rubbing branches, and weak or damaged shoots and stems. Thin out overcrowded shoots, cutting several back to the base to allow young, vigorous regrowth. Remove the tips of young shoots to encourage the growth of flowering sideshoots.

# Fuchsia berry

**Level 2** moderate

*Fuchsia species and cultivars*

While fuchsias are widely grown for their attractive flowers, most growers have yet to discover the appeal of their berries. All types bear edible berries, but size and flavor vary greatly. *Fuchsia* 'Genii' and *F. magellanica* produce superior-tasting berries, and the cultivar 'Fuchsiaberry' has been specially selected for its fruits.

## What is it?

Native to mountainous parts of New Zealand and Central and South America, fuchsias are flowering shrubs ranging in cold tolerance from fully hardy to frost tender. Depending on variety, flowers bloom from midspring to midfall, followed by berries with a texture similar to soft grapes and ranging in flavor from intensely sweet to slightly bitter, with notes of fig, kiwi, pomegranate, and spice.

### When to grow and harvest
Plant in late spring and harvest the ripe fruits from midsummer to late fall, depending on variety.

| | early winter | late winter | early spring | late spring | early summer | late summer | early fall | late fall |
|---|---|---|---|---|---|---|---|---|
| plant | | | ● | ● | ● | | | |
| harvest | | | | | ● | ● | ● | ● |

*Fuchsia magellanica* bears an abundance of flowers throughout summer, followed by purple fruits with a peppery, grapelike taste.

## How do I grow it?

Fuchsias will grow in almost any soil, but prefer shelter from cold winds and a relatively sunny spot, though they like shade during the hottest part of the day. *Fuchsia magellanica* and *F.* 'Genii' are more hardy than *F.* 'Fuchsiaberry', but all will require protection over winter. 'Genii' and 'Fuchsiaberry' are compact varieties suited to growing in large containers.

### 1 Planting

Buy container-raised plants for planting out. Hardy types can be planted immediately. Half-hardy fuchsias should be potted on indoors and, when there is no further risk of frost, acclimatized to outdoor conditions by placing them in a cloche or cold frame and gradually increasing ventilation, first during the day and then at night. Once hardened off, transplant to their final positions. Several plants together will produce heavier crops.

## Cook's tips

### Keep fresh

Store unblemished berries in a sealed container in the refrigerator or cool pantry.

### How to eat

Fuchsia berries can be used as a substitute for cherries, grapes, and blueberries in most recipes.

- Cook gently with sugar and a little water to make a compote.
- Bake in a sweet eggy batter for clafoutis.
- Add to the roasting pan for chicken or game birds.

### How to preserve

Berries can be frozen, made into jam, or stored fresh under sugar syrup—try flavoring the syrup with your favorite spirit.

## ② Aftercare and harvest

Increase watering once the fuchsia plants start to grow in late spring. Feed a liquid general fertilizer to encourage growth until the plants are established. Then, switch to a high-potassium feed, such as diluted liquid tomato fertilizer, to promote flowering and fruiting. As plants grow, nip out the shoot tips from the main stems to encourage branching and further flower production. Harvest fruits when they are fully colored and slightly soft to the touch.

## ③ Winter care

Half-hardy fuchsias need frost protection over winter. Store them in their pots in a cool, frost-free greenhouse, shed, or garage. Leave on as much foliage as space allows for extra protection. In spring, cut back the main stems to within 2in (5cm) of the base, and spray with water to encourage regrowth. Hardy fuchsias can remain outside through the winter, and in midspring they should be cut back almost to ground level above a strong pair of buds.

Level 2
*moderate*

# Cape gooseberry

*Physalis peruviana*

For a fuss-free plant with architectural appeal and exotic-tasting fruit, look no further than the Cape gooseberry, whose sweet-sharp berries are borne prolifically throughout summer and fall, concealed within their Chinese lanterns.

## What is it?

Despite originating in Peru, the plant became known as the Cape gooseberry because it was first mass-cultivated by European farmers on the Cape of Good Hope in South Africa, who grew the fruits to make jam for export. Cape gooseberry is a perennial plant in the wild, but is grown as an annual in cooler climates, as it needs protection from frost over the winter. Plants produce soft, heart-shaped leaves, delicate yellow-and-pink flowers, and bright orange fruits high in carotenes, potassium, and vitamin C.

*The fruit has been given many common names in its travels around the world, including poha, husk cherry, Peruvian ground cherry, and goldenberry.*

**Berries grow enclosed** in a balloonlike calyx that turns from green to pale beige.

## How do I grow it?

The Cape gooseberry is a member of the same family of plants as tomatoes and can be grown in a similar way. Start plants off under cover in cooler areas and either transplant outdoors to a warm, sheltered spot in full sun, after the danger of frost has passed, or continue growing under cover in pots, growing bags, or moved to a border in a greenhouse or hoophouse. Plants also grow happily in large containers of all-purpose mix in a sheltered spot. If growing them in a greenhouse, ventilate well on hot days and keep plants constantly moist. Fruits ripen from early summer and can be left on the plant until needed. Peak flavor is 2 to 3 weeks after ripening.

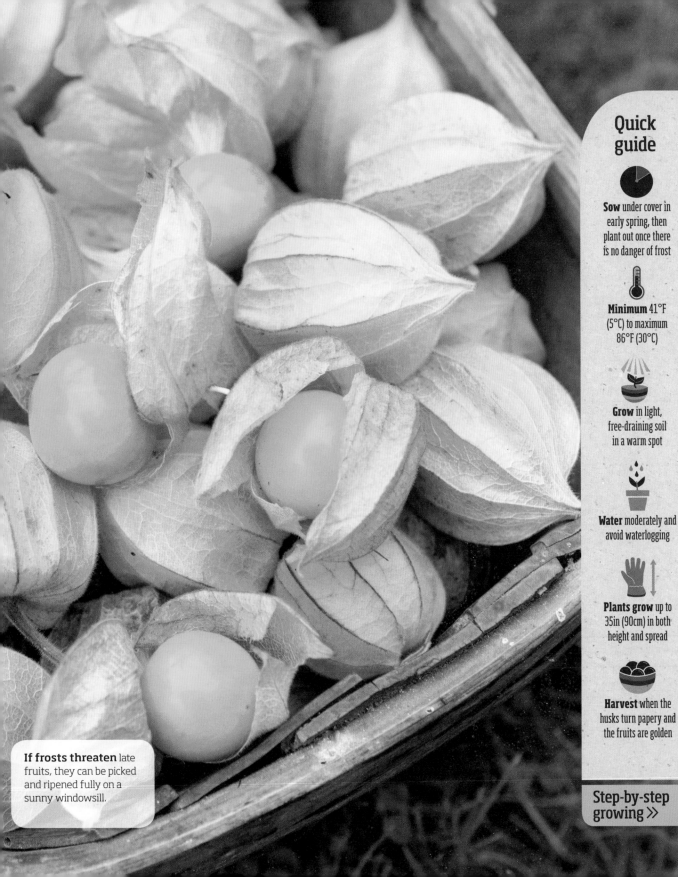

If frosts threaten late fruits, they can be picked and ripened fully on a sunny windowsill.

## Quick guide

**Sow** under cover in early spring, then plant out once there is no danger of frost

**Minimum** 41°F (5°C) to maximum 86°F (30°C)

**Grow** in light, free-draining soil in a warm spot

**Water** moderately and avoid waterlogging

**Plants grow** up to 35in (90cm) in both height and spread

**Harvest** when the husks turn papery and the fruits are golden

Step-by-step growing »

# Step-by-step growing

For a bumper crop of beautiful golden fruits, grow Cape gooseberries in a warm position, water well but not excessively, and aid pollination by gently tapping the flowers.

## When to grow and harvest

Sow seeds in spring, and plant out when all danger of frost has passed. Harvest the berries from summer to fall.

| | early winter | late winter | early spring | late spring | early summer | late summer | early fall | late fall |
|---|---|---|---|---|---|---|---|---|
| sow indoors | | | ● | | | | | |
| plant out | | | | ● | | | | |
| harvest | | | | | ● | ● | ● | ● |

## 1 Sow indoors

Start plants off under cover in early spring. Thickly sow seeds approximately ¼in (6mm) deep in seed-starting mix in trays or modules. Place on a sunny windowsill or in a propagator set at a temperature of 64°F (18°C). Germination should take around 10–14 days. When the seedlings are large enough to handle, carefully transplant them individually into 3in (7.5cm) pots also filled with seed-starting mix. Continue to grow plants on under cover, repotting into larger pots as needed.

**Use a dibble** to help you separate out the tiny seedlings and avoid damaging their delicate roots.

## 2 Plant out

Rake the soil of the planting location to a fine texture and enrich it by adding well-rotted organic matter, especially if growing on a chalky soil. Once all danger of frost has passed, acclimatize plants to outdoor conditions by placing them in a cloche or cold frame and gradually increasing ventilation, first during the day and then at night. Water thoroughly in their pots before planting outdoors at the spacings below.

**Young plants** must be gradually exposed to the winds and colder temperatures outside.

30in (75cm)

30in (75cm)

**Space plants** 30in (75cm) apart, leaving the same distance between rows.

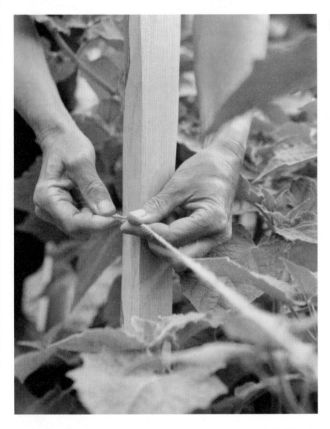

## ③ Aftercare

Protect plants from strong winds with cloches or horticultural fleece until they are established. Pinch back the growing tips when plants are 12in (30cm) tall to encourage branching and fruit formation. The stems are very lax and will need some form of support. Feed a high-potassium feed, such as diluted liquid tomato fertilizer, once the first flowers appear. Keep the soil moist but don't overwater, as this stimulates leafy growth at the expense of flowers. Tap or gently shake the flowers to aid pollination.

**Support plants** with string tied around a frame of stakes, or tie individually to canes.

## ④ Harvest and winter care

Harvest from early to midsummer when the berries are golden-yellow and fully ripe, discarding the inedible husks. Plants grown in pots can be brought under cover and kept somewhere cool but frost-free over winter. Plants in the ground can also be lifted, transferred to pots, and stored over winter. Overwintered plants start fruiting earlier next year.

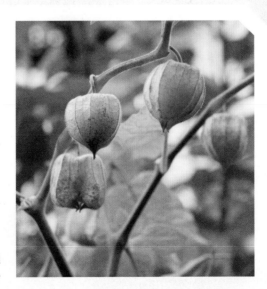

**The husks turn** brown and papery as the fruits ripen inside.

## Cook's tips

### Keep fresh

Perfect, unblemished berries will keep for several days stored in a sealed plastic bag in the refrigerator.

### How to eat

The slightly tart fruits can be eaten raw or cooked in sweet or savory dishes.

- Spread whipped cream over meringue and top with Cape gooseberries, apricot halves, and raspberries for a quick summer dessert.

- For an after-dinner treat, coat berries in melted dark chocolate and leave to dry.

- Combine with cooking apples for a fall crumble.

- Add whole or halved to a salad of sweetcorn, cucumber, and cilantro leaves.

- Mix in chopped berries to tomato salsa for a fruity twist– great with Mexican food.

### How to preserve

Cape gooseberry makes an excellent jam, and its slightly tart flavor works well in dips. Fruits can also be preserved whole in a sugar-and-honey syrup.

## Quick guide

**Plant** container-raised shrubs in late summer or early fall

**Minimum** 14°F (-10°C) to maximum 86°F (30°C)

**Grow** in free-draining soil in a sheltered, sunny position

**Water** young plants in late spring and summer; established plants rarely need watering

**Pruned plants** rarely exceed 3ft (90cm) in height and spread

**Harvest** after 2-3 years, from late summer to the first frosts

# Goji berry
*Lycium barbarum*

{ Level 2 moderate }

A native of China, the goji berry has gained a global reputation as a superfood. Legend has it that the Chinese herbalist Li Qing Yuen consumed goji berries daily and lived to be 252 years old. However unlikely the legend, there is no denying that the fruits contain very high levels of vitamin C and antioxidants.

## What is it?

Goji berry is a deciduous shrub that bears small, trumpet-shaped, white or purple flowers from early spring to midsummer, followed by a prolific crop of shiny, oval, orange-red berries with a sweet-savory flavor. Once established, plants are hardy and vigorous, producing many long, arching stems with a lax habit. Mature shrubs can tolerate wind and drought, as well as salt-laden air in coastal areas.

### When to grow and harvest

Plant from late summer to fall and expect to harvest berries 2 to 3 years later, from early to midsummer onward.

| | early winter | late winter | early spring | late spring | early summer | late summer | early fall | late fall |
|---|---|---|---|---|---|---|---|---|
| plant | | | | | | • | • | |
| harvest | | | | | • | • | • | |

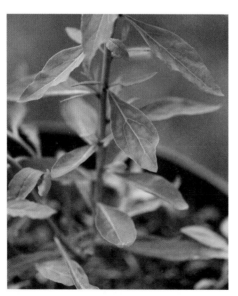

**Goji berries can be grown** from seed, but it is simpler to buy container-raised plants and plant them out in your garden.

## How do I grow it?

Goji berry can be grown from seed, but it is more practical to buy container-raised plants. Plants crop most heavily in well-drained soil in a sunny position, but tolerate partial shade. The lax stems benefit from being trained against trellises or on wires fixed to a wall. Goji can also be grown in large containers on a sunny patio or as a hedge trimmed in summer.

## ① Planting and aftercare

Plant in late summer or fall in free-draining soil enriched with garden potting mix, spacing plants 6½ft (2m) apart. Water in thoroughly and mulch around the base with well-rotted organic matter or forest bark. For the first winter, protect young plants with horticultural fleece. Feed a slow-release general-purpose fertilizer in late spring. Water young plants from late spring to late summer until established.

## 2 Harvest

Goji shrubs will take 2 to 3 years to produce their first crops, as flowers and fruit develop on the previous year's stems. Harvest berries from early summer until the first frosts. The fruits are only edible when they are red and fully ripe. Sometimes berries can turn black when they are handled. To avoid this, place an old sheet or soft bag beneath the fruits to catch them, and gently shake the plant.

## 3 Pruning

Prune lightly as the shrubs start into growth in early spring. Remove any dead, damaged, or badly placed shoots. Cut overlong stems back to a well-placed branch to keep the shrub within its allotted space, and remove some of the oldest wood at the base. Tangled, woody specimens can be rejuvenated in early spring by cutting back the whole plant to a low framework of branches close to the base. Cut back container-grown plants by up to half after fruiting.

## Quick guide

**Plant** outdoors at any time

**Minimum** -40°F (-40°C) to maximum 86°F (30°C)

**Grow** in moist but well-drained soil in sun or partial shade

**Water** regularly to keep the soil constantly moist

**Plants grow** up to 5ft (1.5m) in height and spread

**Harvest** in fall, when the berries are deep purple and fully ripe

# Chokeberry

*Aronia melanocarpa or A. x prunifolia*

This ornamental but highly productive shrub is grown for its attractive flowers, richly colored fall foliage, and lustrous, deep purple–almost black–fruits. The berries contain very high levels of vitamin C and their antioxidant content is reported to be three times higher than that of blueberries.

## What is it?

Chokeberry is an extremely hardy, deciduous shrub from eastern North America, where it grows in woodland clearings and scrubs. Cropping is prolific in moist, peaty soil, but shrubs grow well on most soils, except for shallow chalk and waterlogged ground. The brilliant fall foliage makes it an attractive hedging plant, and it is an excellent compact shrub for small gardens.

### When to grow and harvest

Shrubs can be planted all year round. Harvest the fully ripe berries in fall.

|  | early winter | late winter | early spring | late spring | early summer | late summer | early fall | late fall |
|---|---|---|---|---|---|---|---|---|
| plant | ● | ● | ● | ● | ● | ● | ● | ● |
| harvest |  |  |  |  |  |  | ● | ● |

## How do I grow it?

Container-raised specimens of this robust, versatile shrub are readily available to buy and can be planted outdoors at any time of year. Aftercare needs are minimal: give plants a good mulch in spring to help retain moisture; protect the developing berries from birds with netting; and, once plants are established, undertake a regime of simple pruning in late winter.

### 1 Plant outdoors

Give the shrubs in their pots a good soak before planting. Dig a hole slightly larger than the pot, remove the plant from the pot, and gently tease out the roots. Water the bottom of the hole if the soil is dry, allow it to drain, and then scatter over root-boosting mycorrhizal fungi. Plant the shrub so that the container potting mix surface is level with the surrounding soil. Backfill and firm the soil around the stem, then water in thoroughly.

**The dark, glossy leaves** and hawthornlike, white flowers are followed in midfall by deep purple fruits similar to blackberries.

## 2 Aftercare

After planting when the soil is still moist, and each spring thereafter, mulch with a thick layer of well-rotted organic matter or forest bark, leaving a small gap between the mulch and the stem so the mulch doesn't start to rot the stem. Each spring, feed a slow-release fertilizer designed for acid-loving, flowering plants. Cover plants with fine netting in late summer to protect your crop from birds, or consider growing shrubs in a fruit cage.

## 3 Harvest and pruning

Pick fruits when they have ripened to a deep purple color and glossy appearance. Grasp a cluster of berries and dislodge them all at once with a downward dragging movement.

Plants will need pruning in late winter after their second year of growth. Use shears to remove a third of the older stems at the base, which will encourage new, productive growth. You will also need to dig up any suckers to keep plants within their allotted space.

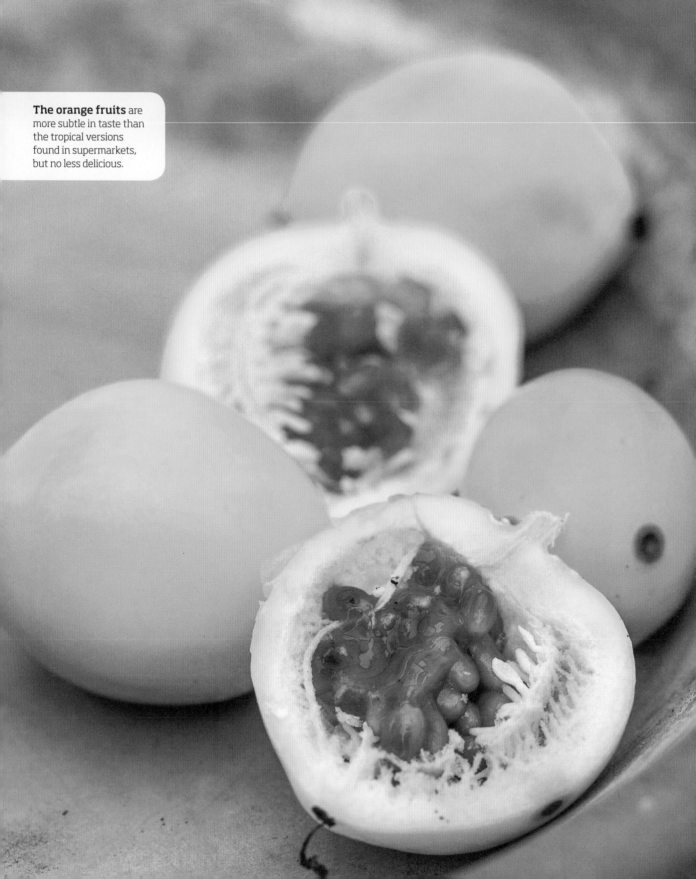

**The orange fruits** are more subtle in taste than the tropical versions found in supermarkets, but no less delicious.

**Level 2**
*moderate*

# Hardy passion fruit

*Passiflora caerulea*

Passion flowers are among the most exotic blooms on earth and plants are often grown purely as ornamentals. *Passiflora caerulea*, whose beauty belies its robustness, produces tasty fruits that deserve to be more widely eaten.

> When Spanish missionaries first saw the flower in the wild, they perceived a symbolism in its floral parts that related to the passion of Jesus Christ.

## What is it?

A perennial climber from southern Brazil, hardy passion fruit effortlessly scrambles with the aid of tendrils. Plants bear large, glossy green leaves divided into long-fingered lobes, followed in midsummer by flowers with blue-banded coronas. From these develop the bright orange fruits, which are roughly the size of hen's eggs and filled with masses of seeds surrounded by sweet-tasting pulp.

## How do I grow it?

Cold-tolerant enough to be grown outside in temperate areas, hardy passion fruit may still be cut back by the cold in severe winters, and planting it in very free-draining soil—even broken stone—will increase the chances of survival. Give it a sheltered spot against a hot, sunny wall, and train the shoots up wires or trellises. Hardy passion fruit also grows happily in a large container in a sunny location. With its striking flowers followed by colorful fruit, it makes a highly ornamental addition to a border or boundary.

**Spectacular** blue-and-white flowers appear from midsummer to early fall, and can be up to 4in (10cm) across.

**Step-by-step growing** »

# Step-by-step growing

Grow plants from seed, starting under cover in early spring, or buy container-raised plants for planting out after the last frosts. Grow against a wall or trellis in a sheltered position in sun or partial shade.

## ① Sow indoors

Sow seeds in individual pots or modules from early spring to early summer. Sow one seed per pot or module, inserting the seed ½in (1cm) deep in seed-starting mix. Put the pots on a warm windowsill or in a propagator set to 66-77°F (19-24°C); germination can take up to 6 weeks. When the seedlings are large enough to handle, carefully transfer them to larger pots filled with all-purpose mix. Continue to grow on under cover, repotting as they outgrow their containers. After the last frosts, acclimatize the plants to outdoor conditions by placing in a cloche or cold frame and gradually increasing ventilation, first during the day and then at night.

**Take care to avoid** too much disturbance of the roots when potting up the seedlings.

## ② Plant outdoors

When the weather is mild and the soil has warmed, transplant the young plants to their final positions in a sheltered site outdoors. Alternatively, you can buy and plant container-raised passion flowers. The procedure for planting is the same for indoor-sown plants. Water the pots thoroughly and allow to drain. Dig a hole slightly larger than the size of the pot, 24in (60cm) away from the wall or trellis. Ease the plant from the pot and gently tease out the roots. Water the bottom of the planting hole and allow the water to drain away before sprinkling a handful of root-boosting mycorrhizal fungi. Plant so the potting mix is level with the surrounding soil, firm in, and water thoroughly.

**Water both the plants in their pots** and the base of the planting hole to help the roots establish.

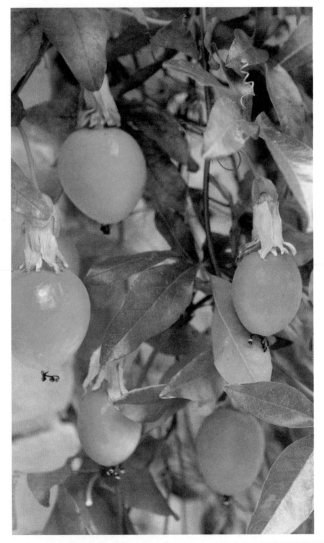

**Fruits turn** from green to orange as they ripen.

### ③ Aftercare and harvest

Water new plants during dry weather, but only water mature plants if they show signs of stress. Feed slow-release general fertilizer in spring. As new shoots develop, train them along wires or up a trellis. Harvest when fruits turn orange and soften. In fall, after fruiting, prune out the shoots that have borne fruit to encourage the growth of new shoots the following year. When the plant has filled its allotted space, give it a more general prune every spring to keep it under control. Mulch the base of the plant with a thick layer of well-rotted garden potting mix or bark chippings to retain moisture around the roots and protect against frost.

### Growing in containers

Hardy passion fruit will thrive if grown in a large container in a warm location, such as a sunny patio. Use a free-draining, loam-based mix enriched with organic matter. As the plant grows, pot it on into a slightly larger container each spring, until the foliage covers the allotted space. Water container-grown plants regularly, but allow the potting mix surface to almost dry out before rewatering.

## Cook's tips

### Keep fresh

Hardy passion fruit is best eaten fresh, ripened on the vine. Fruit will last for 2–3 days in the fruit bowl.

### How to eat

Fruits are at their peak of ripeness and flavor when the skin just starts to shrivel. The outer flesh is relatively bland; it is the inner seed-filled pulp that is eaten.

- Add to smoothies.
- Make a sponge cake filling by mixing with sweetened mascarpone, or use to flavor a syrup for drizzling over polenta cake.
- Combine with papaya for a tropical pavlova topping.
- Spread over cream as a filling for meringue roulade.
- Make passion fruit liqueur with vodka and sugar syrup.

### How to preserve

Cut the fruits in half, scoop out the pulp into an ice cube tray, then freeze. Once frozen, put the cubes in freezer bags for indefinite storage. Passion fruit also makes a superb jam partnered with apricots.

## Quick guide

**Sow** fresh seed in fall or dry seed in spring; plant in spring or fall

**Minimum** 5°F (-15°C); will tolerate temperatures above 86°F (30°C)

**Grow** in partial or full shade in moist, well-drained soil

**Water** only required in very hot and dry conditions

**Plants grow** up to 3ft (1m) in height and 5ft (1.5m) in spread

**Harvest** berries when they are round, plump, and deep blue in color

**{ Level 1 easy }**

# Oregon grape

*Mahonia aquifolium*

A familiar garden plant, the glossy, hollylike leaves and bright yellow flower clusters of the Oregon grape often spread through shady shrub borders. Blackbirds love their late summer berries, but few gardeners realize that they could be feasting on them, too.

## What is it?

Oregon grape is a hardy, low-growing shrub, which spreads through the soil via suckers and makes a great ground cover plant. As its name suggests, the shrub is native to western North America, where it forms part of the understory of plants in forests and woodlands. The plump, dark blue berries are traditionally gathered by Native American people, who mix them with other fruits to sweeten their tart flavor. Shrubs were introduced to Europe in 1822 and have since become widely naturalized.

### When to grow and harvest

Plants take a few years to establish and spread before producing a useful crop of berries.

|  | early winter | late winter | early spring | late spring | early summer | late summer | early fall | late fall |
|---|---|---|---|---|---|---|---|---|
| sow outdoors |  |  | • |  |  |  | • | • |
| plant outdoors |  |  | • | • |  |  | • | • |
| harvest |  |  |  |  |  | • | • |  |

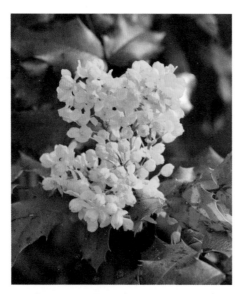

**The fragrant yellow flowers** of the Oregon grape grow in small bunches and tend to start blossoming in early spring.

## How do I grow it?

This tough shrub is widely available from garden centers and is easy to grow anywhere with some shade and well-drained soil. Container-raised plants are best planted in spring or fall and kept well-watered while they establish. It is also possible to grow it from seed, which is best sown in fall as soon as it is ripe, in an outdoor seedbed or cold frame.

###  1 Sow seeds

Seeds can be obtained from the ripe berries and should be sown immediately. First remove the soft surrounding flesh of the berry, then plant the seeds ½in (1cm) deep into an outdoor seedbed, 6in (15cm) apart, or into pots of moist potting mix in a cold frame. Germination requires a period of cold weather, and seedlings will not usually emerge until the following spring. If sowing dry seed in spring, refrigerate for 3 weeks before planting.

## ② Transplant and plant out

When seedlings emerge, transplant those raised in a seedbed into pots, and grow on all plants in a cold frame, through the growing season and over winter, for planting out next spring. Improve the soil at the planting site by working in plenty of well-rotted growing medium, then position the plant in a hole to the same depth as it was in its pot, firm the soil around it, and water in. Shrubs bought from a garden center are planted in the same way, ideally in spring or fall.

## ③ Aftercare and harvest

Generally, these tough shrubs need little attention once planted out, but water them well during any dry weather in their first summer while they establish their roots. Apply a spring mulch of potting mix on lighter soils prone to drying out. Older plants respond well to pruning where growth has become straggly or tired. Pick the ripe berries by catching them in a container as you gently run your fingers down the stem.

## Quick guide

**Sow** indoors in fall or late winter to early spring

**Minimum** 14°F (-10°C) to maximum 86°F (30°C)

**Grow** in moderately fertile soil in a sunny or partially shady spot

**Water** occasionally, keeping the soil or medium moist

**Plants grow** up to 20in (50cm) in height and spread

**Pick** when fruits are plump

**{ Level 1 easy }**

# White alpine strawberry

*Fragaria vesca alba and cultivars*

These white strawberries may look unreal, but in fact derive from a wild species. With a longer cropping season than regular strawberries, you'll be picking the dainty fruits right up to the first frosts.

## What is it?

White alpine strawberry plants are smaller than the garden variety, don't send out runners, and can tolerate cooler conditions. While fruits are lacking in the protein "Fra a1" that gives most strawberries their red color, they are no less sweet and juicy. Alpine strawberries have not been intensively hybridized, and there are fewer cultivars to choose from; perhaps the best are 'White Delight', closest to the wild species, and the strongly flavored 'Pineapple Crush'.

### When to grow and harvest

Sow in fall, late winter, or spring and harvest from summer to fall.

| | early winter | late winter | early spring | late spring | early summer | late summer | early fall | late fall |
|---|---|---|---|---|---|---|---|---|
| sow indoors | | ● | ● | ● | | | | ● |
| plant out | | | ● | ● | | | | ● |
| harvest | | | | | ● | ● | ● | |

**Alpine strawberries** self-seed freely, and you can increase your stock of plants by lifting and transplanting any seedlings.

## How do I grow it?

As low-growing evergreen plants, they make attractive edging for paths and an excellent choice for ground cover. Plants form compact clumps and thrive in containers, so you don't need a lot of garden space to grow them.

## ① Sow indoors

Sow seeds in trays of firmed potting mix or sieved all-purpose mix, in fall or from midwinter until early spring. Gently press seeds into the surface and lightly cover with perlite or sharp sand. Keep moist but not wet. Place under glass at a temperature of 64–68°F (18–20°C) and move to a shady spot or cover with newspaper until germination, which can be slow. Keep fall sowings in a cold frame over winter.

## Cook's tips

### Keep fresh
Line a container with paper towel and lay the berries on top. Leave the stalks on and open the lid in one corner. Refrigerate for up to 1 week.

### How to eat
Eat fresh or lightly poached in desserts or savory dishes.

- Macerate with a little sugar and shredded mint for an easy pudding.
- Arrange on a bed of crème pâtissière in a fresh fruit tart.
- Mix whole into salads; balsamic vinaigrette brings out the flavor of the berries.

### How to preserve
Make jam. The berries can also be frozen but will be soft when defrosted.

## ② Pot up and plant

Once seedlings have a pair of true leaves, transplant into small pots of multipurpose or loam-based mix. Harden off for 2 weeks by keeping them outside during the day and inside at night, or in a cold frame with the lid ajar during the day. Once the danger of frost has passed, plant out in a warm, sheltered, sunny spot with 10–12in (25–30cm) between plants and rows. Water thoroughly and mulch with well-rotted organic matter or forest bark.

## ③ Aftercare and harvest

Boost plants with slow-release general fertilizer or with high-potassium fertilizer in early spring to encourage flowering. You may need to assist pollination by transferring pollen between flowers using a paintbrush. The white berries are less appealing to birds, but cover plants with a net as a precaution. Harvest the ripe berries in late summer the first year, and midsummer to fall thereafter. Replace plants in rotation every 3 years to keep them vigorous.

# RESOURCES

# Index

# Suppliers

The rare and unusual plants and seeds in this book can be found at the following suppliers. Some US and Canadian sources will ship to each other, but some seeds—and particularly plants—can't cross the border.

## US Sources

**Amazon**
*(via various smaller suppliers)*
amazon.com

**American Meadows**
americanmeadows.com

**Baker Creek Heirloom Seeds**
*(ships internationally)*
rareseeds.com

**Bountiful Gardens**
bountifulgardens.com

**Burpee Seeds and Plants**
burpee.com

**Cultivariable**
*(ships internationally)*
cultivariable.com

**Home Depot**
www.homedepot.com

**Johnny's Selected Seeds**
johnnyseeds.com

**Kitazawa Seed Co.**
kitazawaseed.com

**Lowe's**
lowes.com

**Norton Naturals**
nortonnaturals.com

**Pinetree Garden Seeds**
superseeds.com

**Restoration Seeds**
*(ships internationally)*
restorationseeds.com

**Seed Empire**
seedempire.com

**Sheffield's Seed Company**
sheffields.com

**Strictly Medicinal**
strictlymedicinalseeds.com

**Territorial Seed Company**
territorialseed.com

**Victory Seeds**
victoryseeds.com

**West Coast Seeds**
*(US and CAN)*
westcoastseeds.com

## Canadian Sources

**Brother Nature**
brothernature.ca

**The Cottage Gardener**
cottagegardener.com

**Eagleridge Seeds**
eagleridgeseeds.com

**Halifax Seed**
halifaxseed.ca

**Heritage Harvest Seed**
heritageharvestseed.com

**The Incredible Seed Co.**
incredibleseeds.ca

**McKenzie Seeds**
mckenzieseeds.com

**OSC Seeds**
oscseeds.com

**Richters**
*(ships internationally)*
richters.com

**Salt Spring Seeds**
saltspringseeds.com

**Solana Seeds**
solanaseeds.netforms.com

**Stokes Seeds**
*(US and CAN)*
stokesseeds.com

**William Dam Seeds**
damseeds.ca

# Picture credits

The publisher would like to thank the following for their kind permission to reproduce their photographs:

(Key: a-above; b-below/bottom; c-center; f-far; l-left; r-right; t-top)

**18 Alamy Stock Photo**: Nick Kurzenko tl. **19 Alamy Stock Photo**: Garden World Images Ltd / Oscar D'arcy tl. **82 Dorling Kindersley**: Mark Winwood bl. **117 123RF.com**: Yotrak Butda / yotrak. **133 Dorling Kindersley**: Mark Winwood / RHS Wisley tl, Peter Anderson br. **143 iStockphoto.com**: sherjaca. **147 Alamy Stock Photo**: Photos Horticultural / Avalon. **166 iStockphoto.com**: bdspn. **195 Alamy Stock Photo**: Nick Kurzenko. **203 Alamy Stock Photo**: Garden World Images Ltd / Oscar D'arcy. **205 Dorling Kindersley**: Roger Smith.

**Cover images**: *Front*: **Alamy Stock Photo**: age fotostock br, Chuck Franklin bl; **Getty Images**: Joy Skipper cla, Michael Davis tc; **iStockphoto.com**: bonchan tr, cra, juliedeshaies bc; *Back*: **Alamy Stock Photo**: age fotostock br, Chuck Franklin bl; **Getty Images**: Joy Skipper cla, Michael Davis tc; **iStockphoto.com**: bonchan tr, cra, juliedeshaies bc; *Spine*: **Alamy Stock Photo**: Westend61 GmbH t

All other images
© Dorling Kindersley
For further information see:
**www.dkimages.com**

# About the author

## MATTHEW BIGGS

Having trained at the Royal Botanic Gardens, Kew, Matthew Biggs is affectionately known as "The People's Gardener." Writer, lecturer, and television presenter, he is the author of several books, including *RHS Great British Village Show* and *The Complete Book of Vegetables*. Matt is best known for being a regular panelist on BBC Radio 4's much-loved *Gardeners' Question Time*.

# Acknowledgments

## Author's acknowledgments

I would like to thank David Hall, Matthew Oliver at RHS Hyde Hall, Alexis Datta, and Jacqui Ruthven for their time, knowledge, and gardening skills; Mark Winwood for his photographic talents; Jo Whittingham and Jessica Biggs for their horticultural knowledge and writing and researching skills; and Gill, Jessica, Henry, and Chloe for their patience. Thanks also to Fran Suermondt and Lubera for their help, Simon Hickmott for his book *Growing Unusual Vegetables* that first inspired me to experiment many years ago, and to everyone at DK, particularly Alastair Laing and Stephanie Farrow for making this project happen.

## Publisher's acknowledgments

Dorling Kindersley would like to thank Mark Winwood and his talented team of experienced growers for cultivating so many unusual crops from scratch and bringing their flair and enthusiasm to the project:

David Hall - *cabinet-maker and artist*
Alexis Datta - *retired Head Gardener at Sissinghurst Gardens, Kent*
Jacqui Ruthven - *retired Propagator at Sissinghurst Gardens, Kent*
Mandy Button - *owner of Stone Green Oast Holiday Accommodation, Stone in Oxney, Kent*

Thanks also to: Rosamund Cox, Jo Hargreaves, Emma Pinckard, Alison Shakespeare, Jane Simmonds, and Kathy Steer for editorial assistance; Anne Fisher, Glenda Fisher, and Jade Wheaton for design assistance; Myriam Mégharbi for picture research; Marie Lorimer for indexing; Steve Crozier for image retouching; and Kristopher Harper for his fuchsia berries.

**US Editor** Kayla Dugger
**US Managing Editor** Lori Hand
**Senior Editor** Alastair Laing
**Senior Art Editor** Sara Robin
**Designer** Philippa Nash
**Cover Design** Steven Marsden
**Pre-Production Producer** Rebecca Fallowfield
**Producer** Stephanie McConnell
**Managing Editor** Stephanie Farrow
**Managing Art Editor** Christine Keilty
**Art Director** Maxine Pedliham
**Publishing Director** Mary-Clare Jerram

**Photographer** Mark Winwood

First American Edition, 2018
Published in the United States by DK Publishing
345 Hudson Street, New York, New York 10014

DK books are available at special discounts when purchased in bulk for sales promotions, premiums, fund-raising, or educational use. For details, contact: DK Publishing Special Markets, 345 Hudson Street, New York, New York 10014 SpecialSales@dk.com

Printed and bound in China.

A WORLD OF IDEAS:
**SEE ALL THERE IS TO KNOW**

**www.dk.com**